Adventures

In Kinship

With All Life

With all the best, and
here's to an ever - expanding
understanding of our kinship
and oneness with all life
J. Allen Boone

Once Upon a Time

J. ALLEN BOONE began his career as a journalist. He later became a pioneer in the fledgling Hollywood motion picture industry, and was the first to produce a costume picture in the silent days - "Kismet", with Cornelius Otis Skinner.

At one point, he was asked to take charge of Strongheart, the first dog movie star, a high-quality German shepherd. As Strongheart had been trained to be a vicious police dog, he had to learn a whole new mind set.

Gentle Boone was a perfect tutor for the task, but he learned as much from Strongheart as he taught him. Boone discovered a silent language and high-level communication with animals. Strongheart died, but Boone learned that his *qualities* were eternal.

Boone's experience with Strongheart, his part in the total transformation that had taken place in the movie star dog, opened up a new career. Boone was appointed Commissioner of the new Board of Animal Regulations in Los Angeles, and made human-animal relationships his lifework.

J. Allen Boone was not only a Hollywood figure of importance, a lecturer, and friend of thousands, but an author of four books, which endure beyond his human lifetime. His books reveal a consciousness of the oneness amongst all living beings and the soul of the universe.

ADVENTURES IN

KINSHIP WITH ALL LIFE

by

J. ALLEN BOONE

with Paul Herman Leonard

Edited by Bianca Leonardo

TREE OF LIFE PUBLICATIONS
Joshua Tree, California

Copyright © 1990-2007 by Tree of Life Publications

Tree of Life Books,
P. O. Box 126,
Joshua Tree, California 92252

www.treelifebooks.com, www.progressivepress.com
info@treelifebooks.com

Cover design: Exotic Landscape by Henri Rousseau,
Foreground photograph courtesy of Hiroshi Yoshioka

Printed in the United States of America.
New Revised Version - Fourth Edition, April 2007.

Library of Congress Cataloging-in-Publications Data
Boone, J. Allen (John Allen), 1882-1965.
[Language of silence]
Adventures in kinship with all life / J. Allen Boone, with
Paul Herman Leonard, edited by Bianca Leonardo.
    p. cm.
    Reprint. Originally published: The language of silence.
    New York: Harper & Row, 1970.
      ISBN: 0-930852-27-3 [978-0930852-27-6] $12.00
      1. Extrasensory perception in animals. 2. Human-animal
relationships. 3. Human-animal communication.
I. Leonard, Paul Herman, 1910-1999. II. Leonardo, Bianca. 1919-
III. Title.
QL785.3.B66 1990
591--dc20   89-51989

CONTENTS

DEDICATED

to all the animals of the world...
to the child heart that cherishes them, and...
with a prayer that man's hardened heart will melt and
learn Kinship With All Life.

Bianca Leonardo
Editor

A TRIBUTE TO J. ALLEN BOONE

His name was J. Allen Boone. It was not until the time he "changed his world," as the Japanese put it, that we learned that Allen was a direct descendant of Daniel Boone.

Allen never lived more than a stone's throw from Hollywood Boulevard during the thirty years that we knew him. Yet Allen was as far from the modern manias of the film capital's commercial output as an eagle is from a mole. He was a saint of Hollywood, an Assisi in the land of the Silver Screen.

Allen, though fully aware of the "animality" that lurks in mortals, lost no time moralizing about it. He was too busy admiring the natural nobility, the physical prowess, and excellent qualities he so keenly saw in animals.

In a previous and very successful book, *Kinship with All Life* (Harper and Row, 1956), Allen tells of his remarkable relationships with animals—especially Strongheart, the million-dollar movie dog. These memorable tales are not mere animal stories, but demonstrations of his deep metaphysical belief in the Oneness of all life. With a dog for a friend, he made discovery in human-animal relationships his lifework.

As author and lecturer, Allen never tired of conveying his great but simple message: that man can achieve a relationship with all living things far beyond that usually accepted or expected. Allen had cultivated a mental affinity with nature. He never looked *down* on animals as "lesser creatures"; rather he looked *across* at them as companions in the grand adventure of life. He had a cosmic sense which enabled him to soar above all man-made distinctions between humans and animals.

Allen was an explorer into the realm of the unexpected. From his ever-revered Rhode Island mother, he received his basic encouragement for the adventure of exploring. His first job away from home was that of a reporter—and, there is no doubt he was outstanding. When only twenty, he was already an authority on, and writing intimately about, "The 400"—the fabulous Newport, Rhode Island society of that period. He worked on Boston, New York, and Philadelphia newspapers, and for syndicates. As a Washington correspondent, he not only told *what* happened, but tried to tell *how* and *why* it happened. He went through every kind of newspaper work from ordinary reporting to interviewing the very famous. His feature story on Caruso was a classic. Caruso was an abstraction, magnificent but far away. Most persons felt that to watch this opera star was similar to watching a beautiful but distant celestial star. But Allen wrote a story which revealed the man behind the celebrity.

He knew Houdini and the other great magicians of that day. Once Houdini was privately showing him some of his tricks. After a little while, it became boring. So Allen asked, "Why don't you show me how you do it?" Houdini did so, and the demonstration was truly fascinating. Later the famous magician tried this on audiences, and it was most popular. Allen said: "People want to know 'how it works.' They want to be let in on the secret, to borrow it, and use it themselves." Allen was a backstage character. The footlights, as such, held no charm for him. He was forever looking for the wheels behind the wizardry. He forever asked himself: "What makes it tick?" His was surely the scientific spirit.

Newspaper work led Allen to writing publicity for the burgeoning motion picture industry, then centered in New York. When the Robertson-Cole Company, a leader in the field, moved to Hollywood, Allen went with them as production supervisor and became a pioneer in the new film city. Robertson-Cole went on to become the gigantic RKO enterprise.

Allen was the producer of the first costume picture ever made. It was *Kismet*, starring Otis Skinner, and was a sensation at the time. In that glamorous early period of Hollywood, he worked with some of the celebrated stars of the day: Pauline Frederick,

Dustin Farnum, Lew Cody, Bessie Love, and Sessue Hayakawa. Allen was very close friends with Douglas Fairbanks Sr. and his wife Mary Pickford. The three of them did much traveling together. On one trip, Fairbanks and Allen went around the world. He commented: "With Douglas, it was always a continuous adventure. I never knew what would happen within the next twenty minutes. He was as great off the screen as on. He had that same adventurous, spontaneous, dynamic quality everyone loved in his films."

Once during a motion picture location trip into the African jungles with Fairbanks, Allen refused to carry weapons. He believed that all the jungle creatures he met, despite their bad reputations, would be friendly if his thoughts about them were friendly.

Allen admired the American Indian and his ability to get along with any creature on earth. It was his belief that the mental atmosphere the Indian exudes is like an invisible handshake of goodwill toward other creatures.

In Africa, the head of a Dutch exporting firm said to Allen: "Until I read your book *Kinship with All Life*, I never knew why the wild life attacks white people, but seldom attacks the natives." Allen responded, "The natives have a mental rapport with the animals. With those who know it and practice it, there is an interrelating oneness between the man and the creature. I have to be right myself mentally to experience it."

Allen's animal books are unusual. Most other animal books are objective. They tell about the training of the animal, about what man does *toward* or *to* the animal. But Allen wrote about the "Law of Reciprocation," meaning that *the thoughts that emanate from man come back like a boomerang. He believed that animals are sensitive to the thoughts of humans about them. He was convinced that man must grasp the Law of Reciprocation before he can improve the world.* The subtle Law is difficult for civilized man to grasp, but easily understood in primitive cultures. In one instance, a jungle native explained it to Allen as: "What goes out mentally and vocally, comes back to one and at one." This communication between Allen and the native was accomplished by sign language and "intuition," or the silent speech which is possible between men and animals.

He realized that many people ridiculed the stories about his having communicated with creatures other than humans. But they did so only because they had not learned the truth that all living creatures reflect the same Universal Intelligence and can communicate with each other when they make contact on the same level.

In the early Hollywood days, two persons changed Allen's life—Jane Murfin, a famous playwright (*Smilin' Through; Lilac Time*), and Larry Trimble, a topnotch animal trainer. Together Miss Murfin and Trimble had formed a company and searched until they found—in Germany—the greatest dog available. He was Strongheart, a 125-pound German shepherd, a combat dog. Strongheart had worked in World War I and was the greatest blue-ribbon winner in Germany. With great love and patience, Trimble untrained him from his combat habits—unthinking obedience, viciousness on command—and encouraged Strongheart to do his own thinking. The dog became a sensation in the movies. He was the first dog movie star—pioneer to later canine stars like Rin Tin Tin and Lassie.

There was a litigation, however, and Trimble went to New York. Jane Murfin also had to leave for New York suddenly, to see about one of her plays on Broadway. In the studio cafe one day, Miss Murfin mentioned to Allen the problem of what to do with Strongheart. Without thinking, he answered, "I guess I could put him up and feed him." Miss Murfin, delighted with his offer, took him up on it before he could back out. Allen had no idea what this would entail or the adventures he was to experience.

"I had never had even a two-dollar dog," he would recall, "and here I was baby-sitter to a million-dollar dog! It proved to be not so much what I could do for him, but what he could do for me. That dog took me over as if he were my mother. I learned things from him I have been sharing ever since. It has revolutionized relationships—my own, and through my books, that of others all over the world. The year Strongheart and I were together was filled with the most subtle and exalting mental adventures."

Speaking out of his vast professional experience in the theater, he once said: "With a few exceptions, I have never known a human actor or actress who could compete successfully with a dog in front of a motion picture camera or a theater audience. You can have the greatest cast of human actors, but put a dog on the stage and he'll wreck their performance. Why? Because something in us turns toward that which is genuine, like a flower turns toward the light. A dog never gives less than one hundred per cent of himself. Can you imagine humans doing this? If they would, a transformation would come over the entire world. A dog is popular all over the world for this reason. He gives of himself; he establishes right inner relations.

"Yesterday I gave a lecture to a group of psychologists," he continued, "and I surprised them with this idea of two-way thought traffic. Man usually speaks down to the lower animals, saying to them: 'Here I am up here with a big brain, and down there you are with a little brain. What can you send up to me?' I have learned that there is one infinite Intelligence moving through all life. Philosophers with four legs, six legs, or no legs at all, can give to me and share with me. All forms of life with which man comes in contact are eligible for this communication in a grand Oneness of the universe. The communications I have had with such forms of life have surpassed all the interviews I ever had with the so-called 'great' in the world."

Allen reminded people of things they already knew but had forgotten to remember. Upon hearing him speak on a certain occasion the head of a university said, "Suddenly I knew that, as a practicing Christian, I wasn't practicing what I was supposed to know." It's the idea of an all-including compassion that most persons of all faiths have overlooked. One is reminded of Albert Schweitzer, with his Reverence for Life philosophy.

J. Allen Boone was a dynamic man. We never knew anyone who could reform so much, yet with never any sense of preaching or "finger-wagging." In the years we knew him, as his hair grew whiter, we found him still learning from everything—up to the very "end." He was constantly sharing the best in him, the best he knew, with others.

His credo: "Everything that lives, even a common domestic housefly, has something of value to share with you—whenever you are ready for the experience."

Paul Herman Leonard
Bianca Leonardo, Editor

CHAPTER ONE

"JUST JOE"

He was one of the finest, as well as the most amusing experts I ever met, in knowing how to live rhythmically and rapturously, in whatever it was that he happened to be doing. With his sparkling energy, his imagination, his sense of fun, and particularly his ability for putting on a good show, both for himself and for others, he was a continuous delight. All his ancestors in the earth scene had been monkeys, and so, of course, he was bouncing around in the form of one, too. When I first met him, he was supposed to be crazy and killingly dangerous, although I was completely unaware of it at the time.

It all began aboard a schooner yacht, anchored in the harbor of Newport, Rhode Island, one that was being used more as a houseboat than as a cruiser. The owner, an old friend of mine, was a well-known retired yachting captain. His wife and two of her women relatives were living aboard the schooner with him that particular summer. Since I had a continuing invitation from the captain to spend as much time with them as possible, I did so. I greatly enjoyed not only their company, but also the animated harbor scenes, the swimming and sunbathing, and the many other values having to do with that kind of relaxed salty living.

On one occasion, after a necessary absence of several weeks, I returned to the yacht. There was no response to my shouts as I rowed near the boat, so I concluded that everyone had gone ashore. Then, to my astonishment, I saw a monkey. He was sitting at the extreme end of the bowsprit. From out of his wrinkled little face he was squinting at me with unmistakable suspicion and fear.

I wondered how he happened to be on the yacht. There was a collar around his neck, and dangling from it was what looked like a broken chain, which only added to the mystery.

As I climbed the yacht's ladder to the deck, the monkey hurried in from the bowsprit, then speedily climbed the foremost rigging to the crosstrees, as only he could have done. Then he moved hand-over-hand along a stout wire brace, with his body swinging rhythmically in various directions. He reached the crosstrees of the mainmast, where he had an unobstructed view of the deck below, and especially of me. It was plainly evident that serious trouble of some kind had taken place on the yacht before I arrived. The deck was littered with broken things. Every chair had been knocked over, one completely wrecked. And what had evidently been a little house for the monkey, was upside down and damaged.

Completely baffled by it all, I straightened up one of the chairs and sat down in it, then began aiming my questioning attention at that monkey above me, just as he was aiming his down at me. Visually, as well as mentally, we were each giving the other a thorough going-over as suspects, and I had the feeling that he was topping me in all phases of it. Then suddenly, and most unexpectedly, he leaped through the air to a long, loose rope that was hanging down from the upper rigging. At varying speeds, he began swinging back and forth like an eccentric pendulum that had no regard for conventional movements.

Watching that performance above me was as thrillingly exciting as it was educational. I was witnessing the superlative, in movement, in rhythm, in timing. Everything that monkey did on the swinging rope was as unpredictable as it was impressive. Not for even a split second did he come out of his exquisite bodily movements. Watching him was far more than casual conventional interest on my part, for at the time I had, as an amateur, been winning all sorts of honors in acrobatics and gymnastics, both as a solo performer and as a member of a tumbling trio. So, every least thing that the monkey was doing in his performance had a very special appeal in my direction.

As the monkey squinted down at me during one of his brief

pauses, I began an equally intense squinting up at him. Not only that, but I started talking vocally to him too, quite as though he had been another human being whom I had suddenly come to admire and respect. I explained who I was, and how I happened to be on the yacht. I told him of my keen interest in gymnastics and acrobatics, particularly thanking him for some of the new things he had just shown me in spring-offs, self-propelled flights through the air, precision timing, body-swingings, and flexible, gentle landings. After a pause, I asked him if he would please show me some more stunts.

As my last vocal sound went upward, the monkey leaped back onto the crosstrees again, and went into an even more spectacular exhibition. The little producer and star of the show walked tightrope fashion, with perfect balancing, along the wire brace between the two masts. Then, as a fitting climax, he jumped to the long, dangling rope that he had used for swinging purposes, and slid rapidly to the deck, not far from where I was, and sat down. As he looked wistfully and pathetically in my direction, I slowly extended my hand and invited him to come and join me. Within seconds he was nestling in my lap, quite as though such things had been going on between us for a long time.

As I gently stroked his body, to which he responded with a kind of purring satisfaction of his own, I told him in considerable detail what a truly great artist he was in perfected rhythmical action, and what a privilege it had been to watch and learn from him. He kept his eyes focused on every movement of my lips. I knew that he understood me; knew, too, that he and I were establishing silent, good correspondence between us. I was also aware that we were beginning to harmonize our seemingly unrelatable twoness into an understanding togetherness and oneness, and doing so from our innermost essences, to our outermost emanations.

In the midst of our sharing delight there were strange and startling noises behind me. Turning, I saw the yacht's launch approaching. Standing in the bow, and doing the steering, was the captain's wife. Just to her left was a policeman. He had a rifle in his hands and was ready to go into instant action. Standing close behind them were the other two women who lived on the yacht. All four were in a state of dramatic excitement.

The captain's wife was shouting explosive words in my direction I couldn't understand, but that monkey did. As a result, he leaped fearfully from my lap, raced up the mainmast rigging on the far side, and hid himself behind a roll of sail on the crosstrees.

The launch came alongside. One by one the occupants came cautiously aboard, each apprehensively watching the roll of sail above them, from behind which the little monkey was peeking down with fear and trembling. The three women began talking loudly and almost incoherently at me at the same time, with all sorts of vehement hand gestures to stress what they were saying. Out of it I gradually managed to get the following. The monkey, already named Just Joe, had been given to the captain by an old seagoing friend. It was a new experience for the captain. He was delighted. So was Just Joe. They became instant and almost inseparable friends.

A short time after this, the captain was called away from Newport for a few weeks on important business. Regretfully, he had to leave Just Joe behind on the yacht. The day following the captain's departure, according to the three women, Just Joe became insane and not only tried to kill them, but to wreck everything that he could on the yacht. During a brief interlude in "the monkey savagery," the women had managed to sneak out of the main cabin into which they had locked themselves for protection, get into the launch, and head shoreward for police help. It was while they were on this mission that I innocently rowed into the dramatic situation.

At the end of a turbulent discussion as to what was best to do under the circumstances, the shooting of Just Joe by the policeman was temporarily called off. But there was a major proviso in our vocal agreement: I was to take the monkey ashore with me, providing it could be done. I was to assume full responsibility for him until the captain returned and could decide what to do with his "crazy pet." The three women and the policeman agreed to leave the yacht immediately. They were to remain completely out of sight until the monkey and I had gotten ashore, or at least had an opportunity to make the attempt.

When the launch finally disappeared behind some anchored boats at the end of the harbor, I called to Just Joe to come down, assuring him that he had nothing to fear as all was well below. He didn't have to be told that, for with his far-seeing outer vision and his alerted intuitive awareness, he knew what was actually going on. But being a monkey, he had to be extremely cautious, whatever the occasion. For some minutes he remained hidden behind the roll of sail at the crosstrees, staring in the direction that the launch had taken. Then satisfied that the troublemakers were completely out of the situation, he came down the rigging, hurried across the deck, and leaped up into my lap again.

For quite some time Just Joe and I remained totally relaxed in that chair, rocking with the gentle rolling of the yacht. As we did so, I knew, and I know that he did too, that our hearts were echoing back and forth, in a mutuality of interest . . . of respect . . . of understanding . . . and of love. Through the revelation of direct experience *I was being gently but effectively shown that life, in all its aspects, is an inseparable togetherness. Is a perfect oneness in knowing . . . in being . . . in doing . . . and in sharing,* even with such animated items as a supposedly "normal human" and a supposedly "crazy monkey."

Then with Just Joe still nestling contentedly in my arms, I climbed down the yacht's ladder and got into my own boat, slowly and gently explaining to him everything that I did and why I was doing it. I placed him in the stern seat, where he could keep one eye on me, and the other on the harbor traffic. Then with our echoing heartbeats, and participating insight and outsight, I rowed us ashore.

CHAPTER TWO

MONKEYWISE

In spite of the many bad indictments that the women aboard the yacht in Newport Harbor had fastened on little Just Joe the monkey, he was a perfect little gentleman in all particulars throughout the entire time that we lived together. After that dramatically eventful day, we established our headquarters in a large fenced-in yard back of the house where I lived. There he had plenty of space and freedom in which to do whatever he pleased, whenever he pleased, and just as it pleased him to do so. There was one exception—when I had to be away, it was necessary, because of his liking for adventure, to chain him temporarily to the little house, where he did his sleeping and meditating.

Nothing ever dimmed, at least for long, that monkey's enthusiasm for being alive, nor the joy, fun, and satisfaction he was able to get out of each moment, as it came ticking into his experience, nor his curiosity in wanting to know the reason and purpose for everything that he squinted at. Unless he was requested not to do so, he usually tried to take completely apart every puzzling object that he could. In those efforts he would minutely examine the thing, not only with his eyes, hands, and feet, but also with his nose, ears, and teeth. Then having reduced whatever it happened to be to bits, he would examine each bit visually, mentally, and smellingly, and finally toss it aside as utterly meaningless in his experience. It wasn't that he was "mischievous and destructive" in these actions. It was simply his particular method for doing his own research work in an exceedingly puzzling world, especially for a monkey.

Just Joe was filled to overflowing with spontaneity and show-manship, and knew how to make each moment yield some kind of dividend in sharable satisfaction. So life with Just Joe was com-pletely free from sameness and dullness. That monkey had mastered the art of avoiding boredom, not only for himself, but for anyone or anything that happened to be watching him. Whether moving along the ground with his unique waddle, or climbing seemingly impossible things, or doing spectacular leaps through the air, Just Joe was always a fascinating as well as thrilling symphony in motion.

It was relatively easy to understand and then companion with the visible part of Just Joe, even though I knew so little about monkeys. My difficulty, at least in the beginning of our adven-ture, was how to identify rightly, and then companion with the *invisible* part of him—with his *unseen* individuality, his thinking, his feelings, his hopes, and with the many other things that were constantly bubbling within him, and demanding outer expres-sion and sharing.

I didn't have to be told that there was vastly more to that monkey as a living entity than either my human intellect or physical senses could possibly identify. That fact was easily apparent in almost everything that I watched him do. My need, as Just Joe and I began discovering each other, was mentally to penetrate his outer appearance and actions, then discover what it really was that was motivating him about in such a rhythmical and delightful manner, and then try to blend my own total best with his total best in a mutuality of understanding.

The more that I tried to establish the right inner, as well as outer, interrelations with Just Joe, the more of an enigma he became. His visible behavior patterns were relatively easy to understand and then cooperate with, but his invisible behavior patterns seemed hidden in an unsolvable mystery. With all my careful observations, intellectual analysis, and minutely sifted conclusions, I found myself mentally wandering in and out of blind alleys, so to speak, and apparently getting nowhere at all, except back to where I had started from.

Then, to my private embarrassment, I discovered what was

wrong. It was I. I was actually blocking my own way by what I thought I knew as "an educated human" but wasn't able to demonstrate in a testing time. What I needed, it became unmistakably clear, was to set my human intellect completely aside. Also my pride in species. Then I would seek what I needed to know about Just Joe from Just Joe himself. So following that intuitive whispering, I made a radical change in my efforts. In all humility and sincerity, I appointed that little monkey my private tutor, and then let him go to work on me in an educational way.

During this effort to become monkeywise, under the direction of Just Joe a curriculum began developing that was as unique and delightful as it was bettering and expanding for me as a human. However, it demanded many disciplines, such as a genuine willingness to be taught by a monkey . . . the courage to follow facts wherever they led . . . the constant practice of humility and patience . . . flexible intuition, with its accompanying inhearing and inseeing . . . the need for keeping my intellectual tailfeathers lowered . . . and childlike expectancy, receptivity, and appreciation.

What made that monkey tutoring so effective was the simple fact that one is always more convinced and helped by what he sees actually demonstrated than by what he merely listens to or reads. *All that Just Joe had to do in order to get one of his lessons across to me was to be his own genuine self, and then let the magic of the universe flow through him.* Having had to listen to so many carbon-copy opinions, with accompanying visible or invisible finger-waggings, from members of my own species as to just how all the rest of us must think and live, it was refreshing to gather in needed wisdom through the persuasiveness of a silent, fine example. Even the instructing example of "only a monkey" with a bad reputation.

Attaining the receptive capacity for being Just Joe's pupil was by no means easy in the beginning of the experience. For one thing, I was too far out in the generally unfamiliar. For another, I was handicapped by all sorts of humanly generated illusions as well as educated and encouraged stupidities having to do with life in general and monkeys in particular. Then once again my efforts became completely blocked, and once again I had to learn that I was intellectually getting in my own way. In all genuineness I had made that monkey my tutor, and really wanted to be taught by him. And yet, without being aware of the paradoxical effort, I had been trying to do all the thinking for both of us. And our monkey-human educational curriculum just wouldn't work in that manner.

At this point I had to learn another needed lesson in the science and art of being in right relations. With all my respect and liking for Just Joe, and with my deep admiration for his skill in knowing how to think himself around in such a rhythmical and interesting manner, I was practicing a serious fault in most of my contacts with him. That was the customary human pattern of mentally looking down my nose at him as "an inferior expression of life." From that downslanting viewpoint I, being a human, was incomparably high up on the humanly arranged scale of living values, while he, being a monkey, was far, far below me as a "lesser creature," and so to be treated as such.

That downward-slanting mental attitude of mine, from my self-elevated ego-perch, had of necessity to be changed. And what I did to help remedy the situation was to set up an invisible bridge between myself and Just Joe. A mental bridge, for two-way rather than one-way thought traffic. A bridge that had to be kept high, as well as perfectly horizontal, in order to make silent communication between us possible and effective. The more that I gave strict attention to my part in this, the more the many illusions, supposedly separating us from each other as rational fellow beings, began evaporating. And the more that happened, the easier it became for that monkey and me to share ourselves in the universal harmony and rhythm of "We-Us-and-Our."

Aside from being a continuously delightful companion, Just Joe was also an adventurer, an explorer, a philosopher, an entertainer, and an animated poem, all wrapped up in "one package." He was also a specialist in demonstrating how many more ways there are for getting genuine satisfaction out of everyday living than those practiced by most of the members of the human species. I shall always be indebted to that little fellow for the many bettering and broadening values he shared with me in this direction, and most particularly for what he privately showed me about expanding my thinking beyond intellectual boundaries, and then sharing in the consciousness of a monkey.

Day after day I would carefully study the lovely and lovable qualities that Just Joe released from his rhythmical withinness into his rhythmical withoutness—qualities that were as pure and as fine in their outmost emanations as they were in their innermost essences. The more proficient I became in identifying the character tone of that monkey and its vibrating relationship to my own character tone, the more clearly a great and eternal fact began dawning over the horizon of my awareness. This: *in reality, there are no separating barriers between one living thing and another.* That innately, Just Joe, I, and every living thing that we could identify were needed individual parts or expressions in the forever functioning of the inseparable oneness of all life. And this, it was also silently stressed, is true regardless of all surface appearances and seemings to the contrary.

CHAPTER THREE

THE LOST LINKAGE

The ground-and-lofty education that I was receiving under the tutoring of Just Joe the monkey was almost continuous, for as long as that little fellow was visible, regardless of what he was or even wasn't doing, school was in session and I was being well taught. The fresh wisdom and knowledge that I acquired from him was as practical and usable in my everyday living as it had been entertaining and amusing in the way he managed to get it across to me. And thus under the guidance of that monkey I was being shown all sorts of new ways in which to *look at life* . . . to *think about life* . . . and to *enjoy life*.

Being a monkey, my little instructor was, of course, entirely without academic sanction. And no association of teachers, it is safe to assume, would have approved of him as a member. But things like that didn't bother Just Joe in the least. They couldn't have . . . not with his independence . . . his imagination . . . his joy . . . his sense of fun . . . and the manner in which he always poured out his reflected best . . . his keen ability in knowing how to let his intuitive awareness not only silently speak for him, but also silently teach and preach for him wherever he happened to be.

Just Joe never had to be taught that being in the earth scene, especially for a monkey, is a highly challenging experience. He had to be exceedingly alert and cautious most of the time, or else! But he seemed to like it that way, as it afforded him plenty of opportunities to practice what he thought he inwardly knew and could outwardly do. Sparked by the desire to understand the real meaning and purpose back of all encountered phenomena, Just Joe was always on some kind of a frontier, thereby experiencing the puzzling, the confusing, and much of the time the frightening. But in spite of all that, he was always trying to go the happy, fun-filled, and sharing way. And such educational pace-setting was most helpful, especially for a human who was trying to escape into larger areas of knowing and being.

It wasn't the least bit difficult when I first met Just Joe to know that he was burdened with a serious and baffling problem. It was apparent in his eyes and wrinkled little face. It was also feelable in the mental atmosphere that he was diffusing. Just Joe was starving. Not for food, but for understanding, appreciation, and love. For someone, or something, that he could really believe in and trust. For opportunities to flow out and share his best, and thereby come into a greater awareness and cooperation with all life.

Then it was that the intuitive whisper came to give Just Joe the greater opportunity he needed, by having him become my teacher and go to work on me in an educational way for our mutual good. It was one of the wisest things I ever did, as the results subsequently proved. My part as pupil and learner in this most unconventional arrangement was first to become properly humble, attentive, and receptive, then carefully to watch every least thing that my little teacher did. While doing so, I had to give alerted attention to every impression that came into my knowing, or awareness, from out of my not-knowing. In those gently-arriving impressions would always be the answer or answers to whatever it was that I particularly needed to know at the time.

The widely practiced method in conventional human education, wherein the teacher endeavors to force upon his pupils certain standardized theories and practices that were first forced upon him, had no place in the postgraduate course that I was taking under the direction of that monkey. It couldn't have had. Not with Just Joe's sparkling aliveness . . . his genuineness . . . his originality . . . and his total bounce. And particularly not with his artistry in knowing how to share so abundantly his joy and love whenever given the opportunity to do so.

The fresh wisdom and knowledge that my little instructor shared with me required neither vocal sounds, chalk marks on a blackboard, or the least bit of finger-wagging. Just Joe always taught, and most effectively so, through the persuasiveness of his silent, fine example—always flowing out with his best and all in every least thing that he did, regardless of whether anyone was watching him or not. And that provided the ultimate in teaching as well as in educational pace-setting. Often, in the midst of that monkey tutoring, I would recall for new pondering purposes the famous statement made centuries ago by Pliny the Elder that "Man is the only one who knows nothing and can learn nothing without being taught."

 What Just Joe and I particularly liked doing was getting into an old-fashioned rocking chair, with just the right rhythm to it, and then rocking ourselves out into all sorts of mental adventures and discoveries. To get the most satisfying results, we always rode the old chair in a slow, gentle rhythm, with occasional variations to blend with our changing thinking and feeling. In those mental-physical oscillations, my little monkey associate and I would first totally relax. Then, as a most important requisite, we got our heartbeats to echoing back and forth in the right tonality, and then in harmony and rhythm with the universal heartbeat. And that would always give us the participating balance we each needed, inwardly as well as outwardly.

These rocking-chair journeys took us out of the limiting egos that claim to separate us into monkeys and men. I would often get into the old chair without Just Joe being in the room. The moment I did so, he would instantly quit whatever he happened to be doing, wherever he happened to be, come racing into the room as fast as he could, leap up into my lap, and relax for another one of our rhythmical expeditions. How that monkey knew, without being in the room, that I had seated myself in the rocking chair greatly puzzled me at first. Gradually I began discovering his "secret." He had never been educated, or otherwise lured away, from using his natural, innate, intuitive faculties—from hearing with his "inner ear" and seeing with his "inner eye." Or did he, through his bones and marrow, sensitized to the slightest rhythm, catch the vibrations of the rocking chair as it reverberated through the house—imperceptible to the human faculties? Our "edu-cated" faculties have been alienated from the kinetic source of all movement. All life is in motion—the universe dances to unheard-of melodies in the symphony of life.

The monkey was pulsing with the impersonal all-pervasive vibrations of life, unobstructed by the human conceit of a separatist intelligence that blocks the free flow. Ever since Adam, symbol of the myth of separation, a false ego has made man stand apart from the universality of all creation—making distances—creating divisions—by naming, measuring, and judging all around him. In this hypnotic grip of self-deception the human considers himself superior to the animal world and other living things, when actually he has fallen below the level, even of *normal* sense perception.

Those who have the humility of a child may find again the key to reverence for, and kinship with, all life.

It is a known fact that our children, primitive peoples (nature's children), and animals are all more alive to nature's rhythm, are more sensitive to environment and environmental disturbances, than are civilized adults. Is it because civilized adults have had their basic faculties educated away or partially paralyzed? Children and animals are more alert to disturbances simply because they are more in tune with the basic harmony of the universe. Children and animals, therefore, are the real pros when it comes to living in tune with the universal, and that tune is played on the scale of Love—a love for all living things—the unifying principle.

Surely, fractured modern man, overcivilized, overmechanized, overeducated, yes, oversexed, and chronically frustrated, can go to what he considers the lesser forms of life to learn the higher lessons of living harmoniously.

"Except ye become as little children, ye shall not enter into the kingdom of heaven." "Suffer little children to come unto me: for of such is the kingdom of heaven"— of *harmony*.

In those rocking-chair adventures of ours, Just Joe and I would rock, and intuitively listen. Rock, and inwardly hear and see. Rock, and specifically know what each of us needed to know, both as individuals and as a twosome. Thus would the edges of my thinking touch the edges of that monkey's thinking. And that, in turn, would make silent, helpful correspondence between us possible. The more that he and I perfected ourselves in that unspoken speaking, the easier it became for us to get beyond our monkey and human definitions and boundaries, and then start experiencing each other, as individual states of consciousness, as vibrant ideas of the Mind of the universe. Our "inner spaces" had touched, synchronized by the universal Mind.

As Just Joe and I continued to share our totalities in this manner, thereby not only discovering more of the wonders of each other but also expanding our frontiers of awareness in all sorts of other directions, the more a great fundamental fact began to unfold. Briefly stated, it was this: that in strict reality, neither my monkey pal nor I was operating with a private and independent mind of his own. On the contrary, each of us, in our current earth-riding episode, was being guided by cosmic Wisdom. We had come through, in a measure—through the haze and daze, as well as the distortions and confusions caused by centuries of stupidly wrong guessing and miseducation about the real meaning and purpose of life.

In this manner, too, did Just Joe the monkey and I begin to find, and then reestablish the lost link between us—*the linkage which ever holds all life together, in inseparable kinship and oneness.* This link may have many connotations. One that comes to mind from my experience with Just Joe is the binding element of mutual appreciation. How we need that in the human experience! Appreciation is the sunlight of love that makes relationships grow and bear fruit. It is the sunlight that can awaken the seed of greatness in another. And it must be admitted that only great individuals can have great relationships. The future of society, if there is a future, will have to be built upon great friendships—friendships between men and men, women and women, men and women, adults and children, of civilized man with the so-called uncivilized, of the privileged with the underprivileged *and of people with animals of all kinds.*

It will be seen in the light of evolution as a spiritual adventure, the ascent of man from the simple animal stage to the complex, with its infinite possibilities. "Privilege" is to be less and less a matter of economic or social status, and more and more a matter of self-evolution in upgrading the *inner* resources—those inalienable gifts that are the true and vital concern of the "inalienable rights."

The young are already beginning, not only to see, but to live this evolutionary realism. Flocks of young people from "privileged" homes are busy working with the "underprivileged" and their children—in a mutual give and take. Some have renounced the status quo of social and economic standards altogether, in their fearless march toward the Whole Man.

CHAPTER FOUR

THOUGHT BAYONETS

One thing greatly puzzled me in the beginning of my adventure with Just Joe the monkey. What was it, really, that started all the trouble on the yacht in Newport Harbor that melodramatic morning? While the captain was aboard, Just Joe had been a perfect little gentleman in all particulars. Then, following the captain's departure, the monkey had gone "killingly insane," according to the captain's wife and her two women relatives. When I arrived on the yacht, during the time the women were ashore seeking police help, Just Joe was again a perfect little gentleman, and such would he remain throughout the entire time that we lived together.

My suspicion was that there had been much more to the episode on the yacht than the three women had reported either to the police or to me. But I couldn't seem to sniff it out mentally. The women vehemently insisted that Just Joe was entirely to blame, that the monkey had been both insane and vicious when first brought aboard the yacht, but that the captain had not been sufficiently alert to detect this. Consequently, they said, when the monkey got the desired opportunity, he had tried not only to kill them, but to wreck everything that he could on the yacht. The police report confirmed this.

But I wasn't satisfied. Could it be, I wondered, that Just Joe's violent behavior was a natural reaction to something very wrong that had first been done to him and was being kept secret? And how, I asked myself again and again without getting any satisfying answer, is it possible for such "madness and badness" so suddenly to appear in a monkey, and then just as suddenly to disappear? Could it be, I even inquired of myself, that Just Joe is a kind of simian "Dr. Jekyll and Mr. Hyde," and is accustomed to making such extraordinary changes in character and actions whenever he feels in the mood to do so?

What I really needed in order to solve the intriguing mystery was Just Joe's version as to what it was that set all that human-monkey trouble in motion. And incredible as it may appear to those unfamiliar with such intercommunicating between human and nonhuman forms of life, I got the facts that I needed from Just Joe himself—not all at once, but during a series of most unconventional interviews that I had with him as he and I rode our old rocking-chair together in balancing understanding and sharing. This was an action in which that monkey and I were able to establish *unspoken speaking between us through the greatest of all languages—the universal language of pure hearts.* We were moving and rocking, in tune, at once moving and rocking together.

During the interviews Just Joe would sit relaxed in my lap, looking up into my face with an expression that always indicated his keen alertness and interest, mentally as well as visually. Then I would begin asking him questions, usually without making vocal noises in my throat. The questions were never aimed mentally downward at him as "a monkey," in the conventional and limiting meaning of that term, but always sent high and horizontally across to him as a rational fellow being. Having asked the question, I would then listen, as politely as possible, with all of me. And then, providing that I was properly childlike and receptive, I would always inwardly hear, like a gentle but distinct whisper, the answer that I needed.

The silent but effective correspondence that went on between Just Joe and myself, during those intimate sessions, was never the functioning of a "superior human brain in my skull" with "an inferior monkey brain in his skull." Just Joe and I, in that rather uncommon experience of ours, were individual inlets and outlets for the everywhere-present and everywhere-operating Mind of the universe—like rays of light and warmth in their relationship to the sun.

The more practiced I became in finding how to establish the right kind of two-way thought traffic with that monkey as a fellow state of consciousness, the easier it became for us to move along together in a mutuality of *knowing* . . . of *being* . . . of *doing* . . . and of *sharing*. The easier it also became to speak silently to that monkey so that he could instantly understand me, and for him to speak silently to me so that I could instantly understand him. He and I were accomplishing, through the lovely and invaluable *language of echoing heartbeats*, a language that is ever moving from *out of the silence, through the silence*, and *into the silence*. But a language, I also had to learn, that can be spoken and heard only by those whose hearts are sufficiently pure for such cosmic intercommunicating.

The information that Just Joe silently shared with me during our interviews as to what had really started all the trouble on the yacht was so completely contrary to what the captain's wife and her two women relatives had reported that it demanded immediate investigation and verification. This I set in tactful as well as unsuspected motion during subsequent visits to the yacht. As part of my "detective work" I purposely said almost nothing at all about Just Joe, from my point of view, but gave the women plenty of opportunities to talk fully and freely about him. This they did with enthusiasm and competitivelike enmity, still regarding the little monkey as "a viciously bad and killingly dangerous nuisance."

As I carefully listened to what the three women said about Just Joe, with their condemning attitudes, I also gave close attention to what each of them was mentally saying about herself back of the vocal sounds. Then gradually, as I watched and listened to their totalities in this manner, and then sifted and analyzed the results, I came into possession of the corroborating facts that I was seeking. Now I knew that the version Just Joe had silently shared with me about the trouble on the yacht was the correct one—that the three women, and not he, were entirely responsible instead.

What I was really experiencing in that special "detective work" of mine aboard the yacht was a penetrating look-see from a monkey's angle into the *secret operation of undeclared mental warfare*—a malicious and ruthless operation for mentally damaging and killing others . . . and that the members of the human species have been carrying on for centuries, not only against their own kind, but against nearly all other living things . . . a guerilla-like warfare that while savage and deadly in its intentions and purposes is usually carefully camouflaged behind "socially correct" outer behavior patterns.

Just Joe had suddenly found himself the point of attack for one of those vicious undeclared mental wars. The women aboard the yacht were his enemy—three women who while careful not to display it in their words and other actions, because of the captain, were constantly attacking the little monkey mentally, with their ugly and destructive ill will.

And here is the hidden plot of it all. When Just Joe was first presented to the captain by his seagoing friend, there was an immediate echoing back-and-forth between them of *pure-toned heartbeats*. A mutual overflowing of admiration, of respect, and of love. A blending of their total best. They invisibly shook hands with each other, so to speak, like the gentlemen they were, and became understanding friends, well illustrating the long-stated truism that *right relations are possible outwardly only when they have first been made so inwardly.*

The attitudes of the three women on the yacht were completely different. They loathed monkeys in general, and Just Joe in particular. They didn't want him on the yacht under any circumstances, but there was nothing they could do about it, as the captain's word was law, and he wanted the monkey aboard. Thus completely blocked outwardly, the women started their *guerilla-like mental war against Just Joe—doing so by first putting sharp bayonets on their thoughts,* and then jabbing and slashing the little fellow with those invisible weapons. Just Joe, who was highly sensitive to the vicious and cruel mental attacks, and who knew from whence they were coming and why, in self-protection became more and more unfriendly toward the three women.

Shortly after the captain's sudden departure that dramatically eventful morning, the invisible warfare between the three women and the little monkey broke out into the open and became visible. It began when one of the women was sweeping the deck. A very short distance away, Just Joe was sitting on top of his little house, but chained to it, watching her with wariness and suspicion. The woman, feeling free now that the captain was absent, began to lash out vocally and viciously at Just Joe, letting him have it with every uncomplimentary thing that she could think of.

Before she could finish all that she had in mind to say, Just Joe went into sudden action with a common and usually effective skill. Taking a deep breath, he spat at the woman, hitting her on the chin. Embarrassed and furious, the woman swung at him with the broom that she had in her hands. Just Joe wrenched the broom away from her and threw it aside. Then he leaped on one of her arms, and before hitting the deck again, had ripped off part of her dress. In frantic terror, and screaming with alarm, the woman ran back into the main cabin.

Some minutes later the three women emerged in their kind of objective battle formation. They began throwing all kinds of things at Just Joe, hoping thereby to damage him sufficiently "to teach him the lesson that he needed." The little fellow managed to avoid each object flung in his direction. Then, as best as he could, he began picking up each object and flinging it back at the women. In the midst of all this, Just Joe's chain broke under the jerking pressures that it was getting, and he was on the loose. The women raced back into the main cabin and closed all entrances. Just Joe rushed after them and tried to wrench off the cabin door. Failing to accomplish this, and by way of easing his resentment at what the women had done to him mentally and otherwise, Just Joe tried to wreck everything that he could on the deck.

Finally exhausted by his strenuous efforts, Just Joe had to quit. Then he went slowly out to the end of the bowsprit, which was as far away as he could get horizontally from the trouble scene. That gave the women the opportunity they needed for getting into the yacht's launch and hurrying ashore for police help. And it was at that point, too, that I rowed into the extraordinary adventure.

CHAPTER FIVE

NAKED BANANAS

The captain eventually returned to Newport, reclaimed his pet, and they moved to a distant city. This meant, of course, that I had to part with Just Joe. I knew at once how much I would miss that little monkey, who had taught me so many lessons about life and the secret of intercommunication between life's creatures, on whatever level of experience.

A few years after my social and educational experience with Just Joe, I was sent to Washington, D.C. as a special correspondent for a large newspaper syndicate. I arrived there with high enthusiasm and hope, but with a handicap that I wasn't aware of. I had been brought up in Rhode Island traditions, one of which was: when a man looks you straight in the eye and tells you something as a fact, you can believe him and act accordingly.

Now I found myself in the wining and dining manipulations of official, political, social, lobbying Washington. There I interviewed all sorts of public people about all sorts of things, reporting what they told me to many thousands of newspaper readers.

The more I carried on my interviewing work in the Washington scene, the more I became aware, to my dismay, that certain important people had acquired the habit of juggling facts and falsehoods. The deception was usually so well camouflaged and so cleverly and subtly put across as to make the double-talk a kind of diabolical art. Ordinarily, once one got wise to this, he would listen to such a mixture of fact and fancy and then shrug it off with a mental yawn of boredom or disbelief. But I was making newspaper copy of this double-talk of professional politicians, and the kickbacks from my editors, as well as readers, was causing me much concern.

How does one really distinguish between fibs and facts during an important interview? I knew that there existed a solution to my problem, and that I would either have to find that solution, or probably be recalled as a Washington correspondent.

No matter how hard I tried with my various intellectual approaches, I couldn't find a demonstrable answer, and the situation was growing steadily worse. Then, in a manner as unconventional and delightful as it was amusing and revealing, I came into possession of "the magic secret."

A vivid memory picture came scooting across time and space from Newport, Rhode Island. The only performer in it was my pal and private tutor, little Just Joe the monkey. He was sitting solemnly on the ground, going through the ceremony of slowly and cautiously stripping the outer covering from a banana, as I had watched him do countless numbers of times.

Just Joe's neat technique for dealing with a banana, from the instant he got his hands on it until there was no more to be eaten, was as studious, as rhythmical, and as precise as it was effective in its results—one, too, that was always filled with valuable implications and suggestions for human borrowing purposes. For instance, I would appear in the large yard in Newport, where Just Joe and I spent so much time, with a banana hidden on me, but pretending that I didn't have one. Then, as part of this effort, I would make believe that I was very busy with certain important things that had to be attended to but which didn't concern him in the least. Never once did I fool him. He always identified my thoughts and purposes as accurately as though I were visibly enacting them.

Suddenly, without the least outer indication of what I was about to do, I would swing around from my "important business" and throw the banana at him. Sometimes its flight would be fast and straight. In other efforts it would curve to the right or left. Occasionally, it would go lofting and twisting above his head. But no matter what the banana's speed or curves happened to be, he never failed to make the catch. This often required extraordinary leaps into the air, as well as perfect timing of his reactive mind and little hands. Then he would instantly sit down on the ground, and with an eager expression on his wrinkled little face, would wait for me to say something complimentary about the manner in which he had come into possession of the flying fruit.

Following this, the more important part of the ceremony would take place. Clutching the banana with his feet, as well as his hands, Just Joe would begin turning it around and around in all directions. He inspected and appraised it as he did so—not only with his hands, his feet, and his eyes, but also with his nose, his ears, and his teeth, as the ultimate in cautiousness. Slowly and rhythmically, he would strip off the banana's outer covering, carefully squinting and sniffing at each part before tossing it aside. Having reduced the banana to its stark nakedness, he would give the fruit an even more intimate going-over. And then, if thoroughly satisfied, he would begin eating it, with frequent swift glances in different directions for possible unsocial interruptions.

Now I had my clue. I realized at once that here was the answer to my burning question. Now I knew what to do with those diplomats and politicians in Washington. The image of little Joe sitting there peeling that banana had in it all the wisdom and action I needed to identify who was or was not telling the exact truth during newspaper interviews. I knew that Just Joe had used on me that very technique the first time we ever met on that yacht in Newport Harbor. I came to realize that Just Joe was always using the same banana-denuding and evaluating technique on all humans he ever met. As an expert in such matters, he knew that both specimens—bananas and humans—had to be completely nakedized, for his own protection, and so he always did so both neatly and effectively.

To get the key to the men-monkey-and-mind triangle it is important to understand:

(1) that animals do operate with different mental processes than men;

(2) that men, the higher embracing the lower, can voluntarily include the wave length of the "minds" in the animal world;

(3) that both are aspects of the one Universal Mind; and

(4) that therein lies both the variety and the unity of mental activity from the lowest creatures, via monkeys, to men.

Little Just Joe was in explicit possession of what can be called "the reactive mind." He could not consciously remember even so simple a fact that only the inside of the banana was edible and that the skin was unfit for food. He had to go through the whole sensory process each time he came face-to-face with a banana. The advantage in this was that Just Joe's senses were kept utterly alert. The human, in his reliance upon memory and reasoning, leaves behind his reactive mind and tucks it away in the unconscious and allows his senses to become dull and his basic naturalness atrophied.

For all practical purposes, one marketable banana is much like another. Not so with humans. On the surface, and more so underneath, they retain vast varieties in personality. The conclusion is that a good reporter will keep his senses and the channels of his perception as keen and open when he meets a politician to interview as Just Joe did face-to-face with a new banana.

It is the pitfall of our species to let reliance on memory and "reasonableness" become fossilized into pet patterns that replace original and creative thinking. Men and women with patternized minds are forever busy and forever frustrated in trying to fit everyone they meet into these prefabricated patterns of the noncreative mind. This is, of course, fatal to the whole realm of relationships that could be so spontaneous, beautiful, fruitful, and satisfying for all of us.

CHAPTER SIX

TRANSPARENCIES

The endeavor to borrow and then practice the denuding and evaluating technique that Just Joe the monkey had so successfully used on humans as well as on bananas set an assortment of adventures in motion that were as unpredictable as they were intimately revealing. The adventures began when I decided to try out that monkey method on myself. I stripped my own self mentally naked—reduced me to my bare essences. Then I took an honest and appraising squint at what was going on deep down in my thinking and character that motivated my vocal sounds as well as other channels of expression. This enabled me to know more about myself, all the way through—a right preparation before going to work on others in the same manner.

One day, as I continued with this strictly *private* detective work that had to do with my unseen individuality and what went on therein, I was gently reminded, "from out of nowhere," of a most important and needed bit of wisdom. It was tucked inside nine words that I had read many times before but had forgotten to remember. For my own greater good they now came back to me: "Blessed are the empty, for they shall be filled."

At this point it became abundantly clear to me why I was so far behind Just Joe the monkey in being able to identify accurately what others were invisibly up to, back of their outer appearances, vocal sounds, and other actions. I wasn't sufficiently empty. Was too full of myself. Was overstuffed with my own beliefs, supposings, and opinions. Consequently, there wasn't sufficient room within me for much of anything else to get in. And it had to get inside first, like a seed, before it could expand me into greater understanding . . . certainty . . . experience . . . and usefulness.

To remedy this, I formulated three disciplines for myself. The first: try to keep myself as empty as possible, so there would always be plenty of room for fresh wisdom and knowledge to flow in. The second: try to function more with the childlike attitude, with its integrated genuineness . . . its humility . . . its willingness to be taught by everything . . . its natural receptivity . . . and its enthusiasm for sharing. And the third: to listen more attentively to intuitive whisperings, with their accompanying unfoldments, as that little monkey had so instinctively and expertly done throughout the time that he and I had lived together.

Thus for my greater good and expansion, and with a delightful blending of whimsy and reality flavoring it, did I start along the unique educational trail of seeking to become somewhat *less* of a human, and somewhat *more* of a human. It was "monkey business" at its topmost levels. It also afforded exceptional opportunities for mentally rising above human densities, with their pet illusions and chronic confusions. Then I experienced the fun and satisfaction of finding the real meaning and purpose in each encountered component of life—even when that component happened to be a monkey who wasn't physically present at the time. But it was an effort that demanded the strictest secrecy and discipline at the time because of the surrounding "squinting eyes and bending bows."

As part of the adventurous quest, I always tried to keep my concept of Just Joe completely outside and above all conventional human opinions having to do with monkeys. I tried to think of him only in his best qualities, as an individual and unlimited state of consciousness, rather than as a very limited biological item inside a little furry skin casing. The more I did this, even though we seemed to be separated by time and space, the more aware I became of our inseparability as mental fellow beings in the forever kinship and oneness of all life, presided over by the one Mind. I became more aware, too, that regardless of all human opinions and seemings to the contrary, Just Joe and I were illimitable ideas, needed in the eternally functioning plan and divine purpose.

When Just Joe and I lived together in Newport, experiencing the delight of beginning to discover each other in our totalities, my thinking about him, as well as my experience with him, had been mostly objective. But quite some time afterward, in Washington, I began to know him more subjectively. I was finding a more realistic way to identify with him mentally and spiritually, beyond obstructing physicality. The more I succeeded in this, the more Just Joe began disappearing from my consciousness as "a monkey" in the restricting biological meaning of that term, and the more he began appearing there in his real nature, as an idea— a cooperating idea.

From that more inclusive and realistic point of recognition it became increasingly easier to understand how it was that that monkey always seemed to know whatever he needed to know, whenever he needed to know it. It was survival consciousness. This he had without the least bit of education, without needing to read "how-to" books about it. The "secret" of it—as I had somewhat sniffed out before—was as simple as it was profound and effective. *Just Joe had not been dependent upon a private, independent, and separate mind of his own to tell him what to do and when and how to do it. He functioned as a reflection, or expression, of the Mind of the universe. He did this as naturally and as easily as breathing.* He was in full possession of "the reactive mind," something we analytically-minded humans have left behind, to our private and collective hurt. It is difficult for most humans to understand this "reactive mind." It is lost along the intellectually fogged-up earth levels, except to those with eyes to see and hearts to understand.

The common practice of most humans is to separate, judge, and evaluate—from an ego position—then deal with one another almost entirely from externals. They are busy trying to create impressions—by outwardly displayed personality effects, by vocal sounds, by visual sights. "How much have they got?" is an ever recurring question. Not so, however, with Just Joe the monkey. Being the smart little philosopher that he was, he always insisted, as a preliminary and protective action, upon finding out just what was going on behind the scenes . . . what was invisibly motivating all phases from behind the fronting that the observed human was putting on for the occasion. Joe always managed to acquire this intimate information through his effective detective work, in mentally sniffing-out supposedly well-concealed motives and purposes. With those inner facts at his disposal, he could best react to the situation outwardly.

Just Joe, I was now coming more clearly to understand, had always depended upon his inborn, natural and wisdom-reflecting intuition for whatever he needed to know and do. He had listened as best he could to the gentle inner whisperings of the universal Mind. He watched humans inwardly as well as outwardly, at one and the same time.

The more that I pondered those interesting and revealing facts the more obvious it became why it was that Just Joe had had to use his denuding skill on humans as well as on bananas. It was to distinguish between the good and the bad in each specimen, for his own protection. With a banana, he carefully and studiously peeled off the outer covering to know what the hidden fruit was like. With a human he mentally, and with more studious care, peeled off all the latter's outer personality effects to see what he was really like on the inside. Then with those inner facts at his disposal, he knew how best to react in all cases.

Without ever having been taught anything about it, Just Joe, I now recalled with new interest, had always moved in harmony and rhythm with a powerful universal law. It is a law that most humans have forgotten to remember, to their great disadvantage, especially in their contacts with other living things. It is a law that has been well translated into these words: *Inner causes of necessity produce outer effects*, and these effects must of necessity declare the exact nature, reason, and purpose of those inner causes. Unless they do, the effects are phony, which is not difficult to detect with the inner eye.

Just Joe had always been a keen observer and practitioner of the potent and far-reaching rule of cause-and-effect. He had applied this rule instinctively in every visual, mental, and physical contact that he made. He always mentally squinted through every observed outer effect and deep into its inner causes, and he did this most intensely.

The various dualistic humans who happened to come within his range of awareness—those who were often pretending to be one kind of person on the outside, but actually were the opposite on the inside, and that, for personally gainful reasons—were stripped to their cores, like Just Joe's bananas.

As I reached this point in my inner listening and hearing, there was a profound silence for some minutes. Then suddenly, as a fitting climax to the occasion, some precious wisdom came gently gliding back again into my memory, wisdom that had a most significant bearing on what I had been rethinking about little Just Joe and his amazing skill in evaluating humans in their totalities. It was wisdom that had been uttered centuries ago by the far-visioning philosopher Plotinus. And what that rare one pulled out of the generally unfamiliar at the time, for sharing purposes, was this: "In the intellectual world everything is transparent, and all the essences see one another and interpenetrate one another in the most intimate depths of their natures."

CHAPTER SEVEN

DEEP SEE-GOING

It was at that point that I decided to make a radical change in my newspaper reporting methods. I would borrow the denuding and evaluating techniques that Just Joe had used so successfully and begin using it on my celebrities.

Most newspaper reporting follows a more-or-less common pattern, pivoting around the objective rather than the subjective. It is a writing mold geared to the superficial and sensational. While interviewing, the reporter's interest is generally concentrated on the outer act that the celebrity is putting on for the occasion. The average reporter, with a trained nose for news, is like a bird dog. He is alert for anything that will appeal to the crowd-minded and imitators, stir up their feelings and imaginations, and then astonish and shock them.

Up to the time of my Washington assignment, most of my newspaper work had been along that line of surface stuff that is supposed to sell papers. But now, in Washington, with a dawning sense of responsibility toward my readers, considering the political significance of my interviews, I was compelled to become more subjective in what I was looking at, listening to, and then writing about. This meant to listen with the inner ear as well as the outer ear, to listen *through,* which is to Listen 100 per cent. It meant to *listen to the thought quality in the voice of the one who was speaking.* In this way, I was keyed to discovering the character of the man I was facing as reporter. It was Disraeli, British statesman, who said: *"There is no index to character so sure as the voice."*

Listening 100 per cent was the "chief fundamental" of the inspired "Adult Re-education" work via voice training, the work of Emma Dunn, as set forth in her book *Thought Quality in the Voice,* appearing first as a series in *The Christian Science Monitor*. Her many years of teaching the rules of verbal inspiration—showing that inspiration has its rules—was to benefit many public lecturers and to influence untold numbers of students both in the United States and Great Britain. While not on lecture tours, she was playing mother parts to Gary Cooper, Lew Ayres (Dr. Kildare series, with Lionel Barrymore), and many other parts in Hollywood, where both of us had finally settled. I had first met her, in line of duty, when interviewing her for a Kansas City paper as the outstanding star of the David Belasco Theatre, on tour. So deeply was I impressed by the utter sincerity of the woman in her, and the utter artistry of her performances (she played ancient Ase at the age of eighteen to Richard Mansfield's *Peer Gynt*), that I gave her the title of "Eleanor Duse of America." We remained lifelong friends.

Listening 100 per cent also implies "listening" with the eyes, to watch for facial expressions which sometimes contradict what the voice says out loud. It means to become discerning to the way in which a person moves—to get a feel for the rhythm of another human being. Of course, all this was natural to Just Joe, but it seems that humans, with their sensibilities dulled and the "portals of their perception" clogged with secondary fractured and unrelated bits of misinformation (thanks largely to our contemporary educational system), have to be retrained or learn how to retrain themselves, to find out what's going on behind the scenes. The youth of today seem to understand all this when they talk about "good vibrations" and "bad vibrations." They say "vibes" colloquially.

During the time that Just Joe and I lived together in Newport, various kinds of people came to call. The instant one of them arrived for the first time, my little associate would always quit whatever he happened to be doing and focus his entire attention on the "suspect." For "suspect" the visitor definitely was to the monkey until he had been cleared by monkey "intelligence." Within seconds, and often with no more than a sweeping glance, Just Joe would have mentally added and subtracted the "suspect" into a correct total. Then, having processed the visitor, and with continuing alerted caution, he was poised for what he knew was apt to follow.

What was it that so swiftly took place in him, in a kind of animal computer process of the "reactive mind?" What sort of information did Just Joe the monkey feed into his inbuilt computer to get such amazingly correct answers about the totality of any specific human—information that served as a basis of unerring, unequivocal, and uncompromising reactions? I was puzzled. Why was it that we humans, as a whole, with all our boasted superiority and strut, were not more proficient in matters of this kind for our own greater good?

At first, the more that I explored and pondered Just Joe's "intelligence," along with the remarkable things that I had watched him accomplish with it, the more of an enigma he became. What all along puzzled me was how it ever came to be, in the "plan of things," that a supposedly inferior form of life like that monkey was so far ahead of me, a supposedly vastly superior form of life in so many important things having to do with our everyday living. And most particularly, how was it that Just Joe had acquired such far-beyond-human ability in knowing how to move his body about as he did, with such superlative coordination, agility, speed, harmony, rhythm, fun, satisfaction, and sharable delight?

Obviously, there was much more that I needed to learn about monkeys in general, and Just Joe in particular. But how to go about it in a practical rather than theoretical way? Just Joe, with his ability to teach through the persuasiveness of his silent, fine example was no longer physically present. And there was no one among the members of my own species that I dare consult about such an unconventional situation. Then suddenly, from out of the proverbial blue, a plan suggested itself. I decided to take all intellectual clamps off my thinking. With the memory of Just Joe leading the way, and my intuitive faculties wide open to receive, I would carefully listen to what was inwardly whispered to me, and then follow that whispering, regardless of where it led.

Although I set the plan into immediate motion, I didn't get far with it, except into more bewildering uncertainties. I wondered what was causing the obstruction. Then as had happened once before in a similar predicament, I began to find out. *It was I again!* No one else, nothing else. I had forgotten to take the intellectual clamps sufficiently off my habitual thinking. As a result, I was intellectually groping about in the wilderness of the suppositional, the delusive, and the unreal. I had been trying to gather in fresh and needed wisdom, by way of expanding my awareness, with an already made-up human mind—caught in its own intellectualizations and rationalizations. As a result, I had fogged-up the entire situation for myself.

At this point in the exploratory adventure, I was abruptly knocked off my self-elevated ego perch, hitting the bottom of my state of awareness with a thud that still reverberates in consciousness. It was as dramatic as it was bewildering. It was also, I subsequently came to find, one of the best things that ever happened to me. For having thus been reduced to a "lowly and meek" state of mind, in the cosmic significance of those two wonderful terms, I found myself in a position where I had to begin thinking and living anew. I had reached the bottom of the valley. Now I had myself definitely heading toward "the mount of vision" where one can begin to see creation as the Creator sees it.

The more I succeeded in expanding my outlook, actions and experience in the direction of "the mount of vision," the more I found myself moving through a fascinating as well as most illuminating and revealing paradox. Only as one humbly descends with all of himself into the valley of humility can he possibly ascend, with all of himself—through "the mist that went up from the earth"—to "the mount of vision." Here we can find the enduring harmony, peace, joy, and satisfaction that we have long been seeking in vain, by striving for effects rather than by searching for causes. We are living too much on the fringe of ourselves, floundering about, fractured and frustrated, in mere superficialities, instead of being at home *inside* first.

I had begun, at last, to lay hold of this precious gift of man, the creative imagination—rooted in a redemption of the senses. This is something the computer will never have. It implies a deeper sense of awareness and appreciation, tangibly companioned by deeper *breathing,* which is synonymous with deeper *thinking,* and analogous to a state of inspiration (*in-spirare,* L. to be in breath). I had succeeded, to some extent, in cleansing the channels of perception. It was William Blake, the great English mystic poet and artist, who had written: "If the portals of the perceptions were cleansed, everything would appear as it really is—infinite."

CHAPTER EIGHT

SECRET OPERATION

Of the countless numbers of various kinds of people that I interviewed, not only in Washington but subsequently all over the world, not one of them even remotely suspected that he was being monkey-processed. He was being stripped mentally naked, for inner as well as outer evaluating purposes, and for more accurate reporting. Nor were any of them ever aware, as they talked fully, freely, and usually flatteringly about themselves, that they were unconsciously parading back and forth in front of me, in a state of complete mental nudity—like an animated but completely stripped banana.

With all their intellectual equipment, their opportunities for observation and experience, and their pride and satisfaction with themselves, almost all of those many hundreds of interviewed people had failed to discover the most important fact about themselves. Their thinking and feelings, as well as their motives and purposes, were actually as much on display, and more so, than anything they were doing, or could do, to outer appearances.

The more diligently I used Just Joe's banana technique, the easier it became mentally to strip off the usually cleverly-managed personality effects and wrappings of the one being interviewed. Then I noted what was inwardly causing his outwardly expressed vocal sounds and other modes of expression. This made it easy to add and subtract him into his correct total. Then I could write about him as such, rather than in mere fragments of a displayed personality. All of this continuously illustrated, with all sorts of surprising revelations, the wisdom-warning sounded long ago by "the great Galilean" when he said: "There is nothing covered, that shall not be revealed, nor hid, that shall not be known."

It wasn't necessary to depend upon any intellectual efforts of my own in order to make in-depth interviewing with the banana technique the success it became. What I had to do was to set my human intellect aside and substitute for it the right inner and outer monkey attitude. From that point of vantage, and with all of me as wide open to receive as possible, I would intuitively watch and listen. Then, providing I was sufficiently attentive and receptive, the withinness of the one being watched and interviewed for publication would begin silently to emerge and reveal itself. This was done through every vocal sound, every physical gesture, and everything else that he did, or omitted to do.

The more that I got into the continuously revealing adventure, with my monkey-borrowed banana technique, the better acquainted I became with an important but much-overlooked language—that of *unspoken speaking*. This is a language that the wise ancients were highly effective in using, not only with one another but with all other living things, too—a language which, in its purity and soundlessness, contains the utmost in expression . . . loveliness . . . eloquence . . . scope . . . potency . . . and results. It is a language that is as easy to speak and hear across great distances as it is in intimate closeness. But it is a language, too, that can cause incalculable damage whenever it is spoken from an impure heart.

This unspoken language I found most important to watch carefully in subsequent contacts that I made with the various minds of animals, birds, snakes, insects, and other nonhuman forms of life. Every one of those nonhuman fellows, I came to discover, began hearing my unspoken speaking, and especially what I was silently saying about him, the instant that we made visual contact with one another. Then having accurately heard what I was inwardly saying, had reacted accordingly, each in its own particular way. Until I had learned better, this caused me to blame them for the things I myself had mentally started and was keeping in motion—just as the three women had done.

Just Joe's banana technique became ever more helpful as it gently but effectively revealed to me the inner facts I needed to know. As the one being interviewed and I faced each other for the reporting ritual, I would outwardly set in motion the customary ebb and flow of questions and answers. During this, I would listen carefully to everything that was vocally aimed in my direction. But as I did so, and without the least sag in my outer attention, I would mentally strip off his outer personality effects, like the outer skin of a banana. Then I would take an evaluating look at what was invisibly motivating his visible actions and their accompanying vocal sounds.

As my outer observation followed the visible performance of the one being interviewed, so my inner observation gave careful heed to what was going on in the supposedly invisible part of him. The banana technique would be in full operation. Then the total facts about him would silently, but most realistically, announce themselves—in the various details of his biological appearance . . . in the clothes he had on and the way he was wearing them . . . in his choice of words and how he spoke them . . . in his easily perceptible ego vibrations . . . in the mental atmosphere he was diffusing through everything that he thought, said, and did. And so the degree in which his interest and actions were either flowing out and along with life, or turned deliberately inward for self-satisfaction and personal gain, was laid bare before me.

This intimate identification at one and the same time of the unseen as well as seen individuality of the person being interviewed could be successfully done, however, only when my "inner ear" was really open to hear, and my "inner eye" really open to see. Then, providing that the rest of me was properly attuned and receptive, wisdom-filled impressions would begin to arrive in my awareness, like gentle but distinct whispers. And in those impressions would be whatever I needed to know, for correct interpreting purposes, about the one being interviewed. Never once were any of those inner whispers wrong. They couldn't have been. They were part of "the forgotten language"— *that language which the Mind of the universe is ever speaking through all life, for the greater good of all living creatures, all the time.*

Whenever I became sufficiently childlike and receptive in the true meaning of those cosmic terms, I always found myself in rapport with the omnipresent and omniactive Mind of the universe. Then it would become easily possible to hear silently whatever I needed to know about the person, situation, or whatever else it was that required my reporting attention. And those silent communications always appeared to be as boundless in their scope, their value, their meaning, and their purpose as was their eternal Source. It was individual, trustable counseling that was indescribably beyond all sensory methods, as well as beyond all such negations as chance . . . uncertainty . . . insufficiency . . . and failure.

What I was actually experiencing in this unusual adventure were the belated results of the important lessons that Just Joe had been trying to teach me silently throughout the time that we lived together. These lessons pivoted around the generally overlooked fact that regardless of our forms of species identification, the unseen individuality of each one of us living items is as much on public display as our seen individuality. We are all unavoidably moving about, mentally naked, in a universe of mental nudists. It is a situation in which nothing about one's inner self can be really hidden from vigilant observation. This is what that little monkey pal and tutor of mine had been such an expert in knowing, demonstrating, and teaching.

CHAPTER NINE

MASQUERADE

At the end of my assigned time as a special correspondent in Washington, I had the fortunate experience of being turned loose as a roving reporter. I was free to go anywhere I pleased in the world, and to write about anything I pleased—providing, of course, that what I typed into newspaper copy was satisfying to my editors. This, of course, made a reporting experience that was exciting, fascinating, and unpredictable. Almost anything could happen and usually did. And what sparked and provided most of the helpful significance was the monkey-banana technique that I used not only on the people who talked to me for publication, but also on things and events. I stripped them all down to their bare essences for total observation, evaluating, and reporting.

The more this roving reporter adventure expanded, and the more practiced I became in identifying people in their unseen, as well as seen individualities, the more I came to find myself an intimate observer. I could slip "behind the scenes," so to speak, of the greatest show on earth—humanity unmasked. It is the most extraordinary and, at times, incredible show throughout the entire planetary system. It is the unrehearsed show that is being put on day and night, in all parts of the world, by the members of the human species. It is an endless parade of private as well as public exhibitions—drama, farce, burlesque, tragedy, and more—the very stuff evolution is made of. It is an unceasing and flamboyant spectacle in which just about everything that the human mind can imagine, and human bodies can do, becomes part of the production—the onward march of time on the upward path of timeless ideas.

When one watches a performance from out front, within the walls of a theater, one outwardly sees "realities" in words and actions. But inwardly observed, he knows that what he is visually following and listening to with the outer ear is all carefully planned and rehearsed. It is make-believe staged for his benefit and for possible profit. Drama is pretendings that have been deliberately set to words and acts, charged with emotion, to capture and hold his attention, to stir up his imagination and feelings to peak proportions. The plan is to win his attention, his admiration, and applause for this make-believe, and thereby also help ticket sales at the box office. The spectator who views this same performance from behind the scenes, from the wings, experiences a different view. It may be the exact reverse. He sees the manipulations, the tricks, and the many clever devices that are being used to make all that pretending "out front" seem genuine and sincere. That much greater becomes one's appreciation for the mere handful of actors and actresses of genius that appear like stars in the theatrical heavens of any given age.

Most of the world-show that I was professionally watching in my roving reporting was in the nature of a vast public masquerade with unlimited theatrical-flavorings and displays that I was carefully noting "from behind the scenes," as well as "from out front." In these masqueradings each observed performer was using every skill at his command to attract all possible attention to himself, both for ego satisfaction and for some kind of personal gain. After all, favorable publicity is big business. The one being interviewed was often trying to operate successfully with one kind of behavior patterns on the outside, for approving public attention, and contradictory behavior patterns on the inside, for strictly private reasons.

I met quite an assortment of those public and private masqueraders in the various countries that I visited. Nearly all of them were listed as "important" and "influential" in their particular areas. Many had a place in *Who's Who*. My interviews with them were, as a rule, formally arranged for me, and then just as formally carried out. But as our vocal sounds went into the customary interaction for such occasions, I would invisibly go to work with my monkey-borrowed banana technique. Not everyone whom I interviewed via the banana technique was participating in the public masquerade for personal acclaim and private gain— but frankly speaking, most were. It was an easily observable phenomenon almost everywhere I went—a manner of human behavior that was deeply set in a prefabricated success formula: first, acquire all possible external cleverness, a bagful of tricks; then smartly, ruthlessly, if necessary, grab all that can be pried loose and amass it; then, holding on to the accumulation of some sort of matter against all other greedy grabbers of things, try to corner the market; set up some sort of monopoly to milk the public. This contemporary curse, these deadening dynamics of the rat race are in accord with the obsolete notion, rejected by a growing portion of our youth, that it is more important to make a good living than to live a good life—for oneself and for the sake of others. The wise men of all ages have considered this antiquated chase after externalities, this modernism built upon a sound profit motive degenerated into a sick profiteering motive, as a waste of time and energy. As the writer of Ecclesiastes so succinctly put it: "All is vanity and vexation of spirit"—in the realm of getting and spending, of holdup and hoarding. When all is said and done, "You can't take it with you." I am equally certain that the *qualities* we train for, possess and express, such as sincerity and generosity, we *can* take with us—when we change our worlds.

From my point of observation, the cleverly arranged disguises that those public masqueraders were using, in their competitive efforts to outdazzle and outdo one another by way of acquiring all possible wealth, fame, and influence for themselves, were educational as well as challenging. Educational were the intimately revealing studies into human artifice and cunning. And challenging it surely was to have to decide, just how to handle, or not to handle, such disrobed facts in newspaper copy. The interviewed public masqueraders were operating almost entirely in externals. Their values were outer ones, the kind they could identify and exploit with their physical senses. To them the physical and material were the important things in life. All the rest, they believed, was for "impractical dreamers."

Although reporting about important people, places, and events was my editors' primary demand upon me, my favorite method for acquiring unusual and appealing newspaper copy was quite unorthodox. Without any set plans, I would quietly slip away from wherever I happened to be, in whatever country it was, and then go wherever the intuitive winds blew me, either near or far. Then, whenever my inner and outer eye would identify some particular person as a promising one to talk with for publication, I would always do so. In not one of those instances did I know who the person was, or anything else about him. I simply went with my inner seeing and its accompanying whisper—and the successful results always followed as a natural consequence.

Having come into mutually visible contact with the stranger, I would inwardly, as well as outwardly, bow my sincere respect and good will in his direction. To this mental approach there would always be a gracious response in one way or another. Then I would usually ease us into conversation by asking a question about some nearby object that I knew he could explain. This, in turn, would set up an invisible bridge between us for two-way thought traffic. *Our hearts and understanding would be in tune and in time not only with each other, but also in harmony and rhythm with life itself.* And out of this would always come exceptionally fine material for sharing purposes via newsprint.

Since most individuals are evaluated by the customary standard wherein wealth and fame, regardless of how acquired, are usually considered the real signs of achievement and worth, all the strangers that I met and interviewed in this manner were "nobodies at all"—not worth that kind of attention and effort. None of them had ever been considered important enough before to have anything written about him for publication. Nor did any of them have any tangible possessions that would have been the least bit envied by conventional-minded observers.

A delightful and thought-provoking paradox always went skipping along with this phenomenon. Of the many hundreds of people in different countries whom I first watched in action and then depth-interviewed, the most successful ones—that is, those who were demonstrating genuine happiness, joy, satisfaction, and peace of mind—were those "nobodies with nothing." Not the "famous ones with everything." And by an unforgettable turn in the paradox, the most satisfying material for the editor and reader alike, that I managed to acquire throughout my entire reporting career, came not from widely publicized personalities that I talked with professionally, but from those simple, humble, most refreshing "nobodies."

The fresh wisdom and knowledge that those "nobodies" shared with me seldom came from anything that any of them had heard, read, or been taught, but from within their own individual selves. From listening to the intuitive whisperings of the infinite Mind of the universe, and then acting accordingly, they had found themselves. From the natural radiations of their own distinct but unseen individualities they had something genuine to share. From a pure heart each was sending forth his song of himself as simply and naturally as he was breathing—as birds do their song and as flowers send forth their fragrance. There are vibrations as perceptibly felt in their gentle impact as they are easy to interpret rightly after the impact has been made.

To meet with an understanding heart one of those "nobodies with nothing" was always like coming in contact with a fresh, salty sea breeze—experiencing the exhilarating and bettering effects of it. Through pioneering efforts in their own individual states of consciousness, each had discovered for himself how to maintain a maximum of happiness, fun, and satisfaction while riding the earth's merry-go-round about the sun. And they had learned to establish the right inner as well as outer interrelations with the other earth-riding passengers they met—regardless of forms, species identifications, or reputations.

Their "secret" for such rare accomplishments was as simple as it was profound and far-reaching. *Each of them loved living, and loved everything living that he met*, while casting the gentle radiance of his own sweet significance upon things without life.

Be The love you are.

CHAPTER TEN

TOPSY-TURVY WORLD

During my global reporting I had to encounter a human world that was prodigiously on the loose . . . a world rushing frantically through dramatic changes that were often difficult—both to keep up with and to interpret adequately into newspaper copy. It was a period of dense mental fog and accompanying low visibility in which the general atmosphere was saturated with selfishness . . . insincerity . . . dishonesty . . . disillusionment . . . and despair. It was an age when, as seldom before, in nearly all public activities defectives were performing for other fascinated defectives, and being highly paid and honored for it. It was a time, too, that was vibrating to the clashes and crashes caused by an ever-widening breakdown in morals, ethics, good taste, and gracious manners.

Along with numberless other professional observers, my editors were greatly disturbed by the downward-skidding trend in local, national, and world conditions.

To them almost everything was not only in a deplorable and alarming state, but was rapidly worsening. So, as part of my reporting assignment, I was requested to interview as many different kinds of people as possible, and find out not only what they thought was to blame for the generally bad world conditions, but how best to correct them. The private opinion of my editors, but subject to change if they could be convinced, was that modern civilization was not only decadent, but speeding toward a total disaster.

Almost every one of the many hundreds of persons in different countries whom I subsequently interviewed about the disturbing human behavior had ready answers and remedies for all of it. By an amusing as well as a revealing coincidence, each of them placed the blame on some particular personality that he didn't like at all or on some particular group that he didn't belong to or like either. Then, having indicted the other fellow or fellows for their local, national, or world misconduct, the interviewee would generally go into guerilla-like action against them, with hate-filled, damaging thoughts and words.

The zeal for placing the blame for whatever was wrong in the human scene on the other fellow was exceedingly popular almost everywhere. As a particular person talked for publication, he first pruned the behavior patterns of the one being criticized. Then the speaker would make him over into his own image and likeness, and, if possible, control the person's thinking as well as other actions. And always there was the proud implication that the one being interviewed was far better qualified to live the life of the one he was condemning, than the latter was himself.

I was not in entire agreement with the pessimistic opinions of most of the people whom I interviewed. My own feelings were that regardless of all viewpoints and seemings to the contrary, an understanding, friendly, and cooperating world was both possible and practical—not only between all kinds of humans, but between humans and all other living things, not in some vague future, but in the immediate here and now. Just how this was to happen was not quite clear at the time, for I was having to meet a common challenge—navigating myself through the confusions and contradictions of centuries of wrong guessing about the real meaning and purpose of life, and how each of us fits into its cosmic plan.

Then, within a short space of time, I had two unforgettable interviews that provided rare and illuminating breakthroughs in my reporting quest. One took place on top of a lonely mountain in the Orient, the other in a jungle. Neither of the individuals had ever before talked to anyone for publication. As a matter of fact, neither of them was the least bit aware that he was being processed when I went to work on him. Conventionally evaluated, each was not supposed to know much of anything, about anything, that was really worth listening to and then passing along, especially in printed words.

The man on top of the mountain was sitting cross-legged on the ground when I unexpectedly walked into his presence. The palms of his hands were together just below his chin. His closed eyes opened as he heard me. I had interrupted him in his meditations. His smile and gracious bow were a welcome and a blessing in one movement. He invited me to join him on the ground. I did so. As he was able to speak my variety of vocal language, our thinking and words began flowing back and forth in a refreshing mutuality of interest and understanding. His intimate knowledge of world conditions was amazing, and so was the gentle, penetrating wisdom. He was an exceptional find.

For some time we talked analytically about the serious sag in moral and ethical human behavior throughout the world, and of its damaging consequences.

Then I asked him if he thought it would ever be possible for the members of the human species throughout the world to get out of their disorders, confusion, strife, destruction, misery, and the rapid deterioration of human relationships.

He smiled and nodded reassuringly. He had no doubt of it.

"How?" I asked. I recalled, as I did so, that almost everyone else had recommended drastic action against some particular person or group for whom he had a carefully cultivated enmity.

He closed his eyes and for some minutes kept the lids down. When he opened them again he looked across at me, and said in his gentle, soft-spoken manner: "There is only one way in which it can be done, and that is by *individual purification and refinement. As each of us improves himself, he helps the world just that much. As he neglects to improve himself, he holds the world back just that much.*"

That observation will long reverberate in galleries of my memory. And while that humble and almost naked little fellow was never aware of it, his wisdom-filled words reached many thousands of people all over the world—through the printed word, radio, and person-to-person sharing. That little "nobody with nothing," but richly equipped with a pure heart and its corresponding clear vision, had set an incalculable amount of good in motion by simply "letting his light shine."

The second of these unconventional interviews was with a philosopher of the jungle. I had been wandering about in an African jungle, curious, fascinated. Suddenly, a native and I turned the same bend on the same trail, from opposite directions. All outer movements in each of us instantly stopped. Before I could think what to do next, he smiled. I smiled back. We started finding and sharing ourselves in a remarkable degree. From that time on, for as long as I was in that part of the jungle, he and I were inseparable.

My newly acquired friend had lived in the jungle for over forty years. During this time he had mastered, to a superlative degree, the science and art of right relations. As a result, he could instantly establish silent good correspondence with every living thing he met. To him every form of life that he encountered was both an admired and good neighbor, even those classified as "exceedingly dangerous and deadly." And as far as I was able to observe, they were all treating him as an admired and good neighbor, too.

My friend's skill in knowing how to get along happily with wild animals, birds, snakes, insects, and kindred fellows was so intriguing that I began to find out, whenever possible, what he did to make such extraordinary relationship results so mutually successful. It wasn't easy at first, owing to the fact that neither of us could understand the other's national language. So what we had to depend on was an improvised sign language, and alerted inner listening, hearing, seeing, and understanding.

Gradually, through outer observation and intuitive listening, and with no intellectual theories or opinions permitted to get in the way and fog up needed unfoldings, I managed to discover his "magic secret." When he and a wild animal, for instance, came into visual contact with each other for the first time, they would both instantly stop and become as motionless as statues. Then they looked across at each other with almost expressionless faces. For the conventional observer it would be a dramatic and shivery experience—one in which he would wonder which of them would do the most deadly damage to the other.

But neither bodily damage nor any killing would result from that unexpected meeting between those two supposedly implacable enemies. Instead, it would be the beginning of a swift balance in inner as well as outer interrelations. How did they reestablish the fraternal linkage between them? As the odd tableau between them started, that untaught but exceedingly wise little jungle man would instantly go into his invisible but most effective action. His thinking was filled with genuine admiration, respect, and love for the wild animal; so he would identify it with its best qualities. Then, in the same rhythmical action, he would blend his own best qualities with the animal's.

In this manner, those two seemingly unrelatable jungle dwellers would successfully bridge across to each other. Through *the universal language of echoing pure heartbeats* they would thus establish silent and mutually helpful correspondence between them. Then, *as man and animal carefully listened to the inner whisperings of the Mind of the universe,* they would each intuitively know what best to do about whatever needed to be done. Both as distinct individuals and as a two-legged and four-legged twosome, they would enter the path of peace and survival.

CHAPTER ELEVEN

DRUMBEATS

Three special interests always accompanied me, roaming the world as a reporter looking for the unusual to write about. The first: to explore, with a friendly curiosity, the inner significance and purpose of all encountered phenomena, whether person, place, or thing. The second: to find out all that I could about "the lost linkage" that innately holds all life together in kinship and oneness. And the third: to listen to drumbeats.

I was so interested in listening to drums that I often went far out of my way to hear them; the reason puzzled me at first. I always found inspiration in the exhilarating things those sounds did to me all the way through my body and spirit. No other instruments were needed upon those occasions for me—just a single drum, or an assortment of them. There was one exception: whenever I was privileged to "sit in the lap of Mother Earth" with some of my American Indian friends, I would also listen to exquisitely lovely sound poetry produced by a flute and drum together.

Although I was unable to explain the mystery of it, I could always sense a fascinating and revealing language spoken through the drumbeats that I heard. It is language filled with important tonal symbols, and their meanings are the most primitive. Whenever any kinds of drummings were to take place, I always tried to be there. Then, figuratively speaking, I would sit at the feet of the performers, as attentive as possible.

Each drummer I listened to expressed values in living that were bubbling deep within himself and demanding outer expression for sharing. Each of them was thumping his feelings through his instrument, in the universal language of the drumbeat. Here is an ancient method of communicating that vibrates with the basic rhythm of all languages, that of pure sound. It is a language impossible to understand unless one's intellect is turned off and his intuitive faculties, his instincts, and his primitive feelings are turned full-on.

Could it be that the drumbeat first originated in mankind to copy the heartbeat?

Many of the drums that I listened to with fascinated interest were sounded across to me in various parts of the United States. In American Indian territory the drum has always played an important ceremonial part in group activities. I also listened to their rhythmic beat in many European, African, and Oriental countries. I heard drumbeats on faraway and almost deserted mountains, in jungles, and on lovely, fragrant South Sea Islands. I heard the vibrant pulsebeat in many places where people were experiencing perfect coordination through the joy-filled rhythms of the beating of drums.

The drums used during those various occasions were made of all kinds of materials, and were just about as diversified in size and design as they were in decorative effects. At one end of the assortment were drums that had been made from tree trunks and were a dozen feet or more in length. The tribal drums required at least a dozen men to lift and then aim them in the desired direction. They were always beaten with padded clubs in order to produce the loudest possible booming effects. At the other end of the assortment were all kinds of small drums, some of them made from tiny shells and so delicate that they had to be gently tapped by a fingertip. Between these two extreme groupings were all sorts of various-sized drums. Some of them were soft-spoken drums for inspirational purposes, and others were loud-speaking drums for emotional and physical stimulation, for warnings, and for warfare.

Sometimes the drummer would straddle his drum, like "Riding a cockhorse to Banbury Cross." From that vantage point he would start his drum saying things for him that he couldn't possibly have expressed in either vocal or written language. More often, though, the drummer would hold his instrument affection-ately under one of his arms, or in one of his hands, or hitched to his body, or slanted toward him on the ground. Then he would translate his intimate thinking and feelings into all kinds of sound vibrations—by thumping the drum either with the palms of his hands, his fists, his fingertips, or by the use of one or two sticks.

Most of the medium-size drums that I listened to were being used at various kinds of social, ceremonial, and other more-or-less formal occasions. In nearly all instances the drums were being thumped for one primary purpose. It was to speak rhythmically and emotionally to everyone present, thereby encouraging them to mingle and share themselves. Most of the smaller drums that I occasionally heard were being tapped by lone pilgrims on the sacred way in Eastern countries. Each pilgrim was sitting on the ground, in complete solitude. As he prayed or chanted or just quietly meditated, he finger-tapped his tiny drum with a gentle beat and rhythm. He was doing so in the effort to express or underscore more adequately his deep spiritual longings.

Quite unforgettable, because of their size, their uniqueness, and the purposes for which they were being used, were the big drums that had been made from tree trunks. Each of those drums had been designed to have a deep, powerful, far-reaching, and even frightening voice. The voice of the drums was usually boomed forth for one or the other of two important purposes: that of communicating code messages to far-distant listeners, or to warn away all trouble-makers in the neighborhood, be they humans, animals, or anything else—like demons or evil spirits.

The more that I listened, inwardly as well as outwardly, to those various drum voices, the more apparent it became how boundless the scope of language really is, and how utterly impos-sible it is to limit language to vocal sounds, written words, or physical gestures. Through the simple but highly informative eloquence of those various drumbeats I was constantly being reminded of a much-overlooked fact: _language is any means what-soever by which infinite Intelligence speaks to receptive hearts and minds_, thereby causing more of the as-yet-unknown to become known and provable.

The perfect climax to my wide experience of listening to drum voices took place on the famous and fabulous island of Bali. Along with a few specially invited guests, I was sitting on the ground in the soft, fragrant atmosphere of a sacred grove. A full moon was shining overhead. The occasion was a special performance by one of the island's famous gamelan orchestras. It was a large group of exceedingly skilled musicians. Unlike most orchestras, however, the instruments used by the Balinese were almost entirely percussion ones, consisting of drums, cymbals, gongs, metal kettles, bells, and many other objects that I could not identify, all producing the most uncommon and fascinating sounds when struck.

The orchestra had no leader. None of the performers required scores. And there had been no rehearsals for this special performance. It was all a natural, spontaneous expression. It flowed rhythmically from their individual withinness into their collective withoutness. For rich and stimulating tonal qualities, for exotic and refined rhythms, and for most unpredictable beginnings and endings, it far surpassed anything that I had ever heard before or could have imagined. None of it was governed by the Western law of harmony. The Balinese performers were completely unhampered in their melodic withinness and its outward melodious expression. The impact of those rare and exquisite sounds transformed all of us listeners into new dimensions of being.

In the midst of this delectable occasion I became aware, as never before, of the interesting correlation that always exists between a drummer and his drum. It is a correlation in which the drum becomes the rhythmical and interpretive, the ritual voice of the one doing the drumming. And out of this dedicated performance by the Balinese musicians were flowing hauntingly lovely and rare tonal values and rhythms.

The intimate affiliation between each of the Balinese musicians and his particular percussion instrument became revealingly clear to me. It was a perfectly blended symbolical action between them, one in which the heartbeat of the performer and the soundbeat of his instrument vibrated together in blended articulation, in the boundless harmonies and rhythms of universal togetherness. It became more readily understandable why it is that down through the centuries, and in every country of the world, the drum is such a greatly-loved and popular instrument.

Those Balinese experts were realistically demonstrating in every least percussion sound they made that drums are not merely instruments for percussion purposes. They are tonal symbols of struggles . . . of failures . . . of losses . . . loves . . . and of sorrows. They are rhythmic symbols of accomplishment . . . of success . . . of satisfaction . . . and of joy. And symbols of many, many other things they are—throbbing deep within the individual heart. They are ever asking expression beyond spoken and written words, quite on the border of the kinetic, of movement itself, the basic faculty of man and his earliest means of expression. Could there be a transmission of rhythmic vibration more intimate and direct—unless it be the rhythm between an Indian rider and his horse to the rhythmic beat of the horse's hoofs?

What added such fine flavoring to the rare music by the Balinese was the fine impact that their individual characters and purposes were having, through their music, on everyone that happened to be listening. It was irresistible. It was also the basic secret for their phenomenal success. Before going into orchestral action I managed to discover that each of the musicians first attuned himself to himself as a living instrument. Then he would blend that living tone of his with the living tones of his melodious and rhythmical associates. And then each of them would fill every instrument sound that he made with the pure, divine sounds that he was distinctly hearing within himself.

Thus with his particular instrument to do the talking for him each of the Balinese virtuosos would thump the exquisitely lovely and meaningful things that were thumping deep within him, demanding to be shared in rhythmical expression. And usually accompanying this, I also came to find, was a longing on the part of each one of them to get his heartbeat, as well as the soundbeat of his instrument, *in tune and in time with the universal heartbeat.* This enabled the Balinese musicians more effectively to become contributing parts in the celestial symphony of the universe.

CHAPTER TWELVE

JUNGLE CLEARING

During my world-roving reporting experience it occasionally became necessary, for my own peace of mind, to escape from "modern civilization." I simply had to get away from having to listen to the members of my own species talk about themselves for publication. My customary plan for those refreshers was to slip away quietly from wherever I happened to be. I would intuitively find some inviting and quiet place where I could totally relax. Then I listened to the Voice of Silence as it gently spoke its enriching wisdom through everything. This put me in tune to moving out of myself and the contemporary intellectual scene and into unity with the cosmic harmony and the rhythm of the universe.

Those temporary escapes provided the needed opportunities for carefully pondering the things that I had been observing and that had been thrust upon my consciousness. We all need time off: for sifting values from nonvalues. For correcting faulty observations and conclusions. For regaining an inner as well as an outer balance. This inward journeying is indispensable for acquiring more demonstrable angles on what life is all about, the why and wherefore of living, and what one should be doing about it.

One of the most unforgettable of those retreat experiences took place in a clearing in an Eastern jungle. For some time I had been footing-along a wiggling trail, wondering where it was going and what would happen to it and me when we got there. I arrived at the clearing. The scenic arrangement of the place, with its exotic colorings, its pungent fragrance, and its cathedral-like silence, was enchanting. It was a fairly large place, encircled by living walls of dense vegetation. Trees of many varieties had intertwined their branches overhead, clasping uplifted hands to create a beautiful green ceiling through which the sun's rays were penetrating with constantly changing color effects.

It was a perfect place in which to relax . . . to watch . . . to breathe deeply . . . to listen . . . and to be silently taught. So I walked in and took possession of the place. Or at least I thought I had taken possession. I spied a tree with just the right slant to it, sat down on the ground, and leaned comfortably back against it. For quite some time my only conscious activity was inbreathing the fragrant atmosphere, enjoying the quiet, and outbreathing my gratitude.

In the midst of this felicity there came an unexpected interruption. From one of the trees at the other side of the clearing a fairly large monkey dropped to the ground. He looked swiftly and cautiously first to the left and then to the right. With continuing caution he waddled rhythmically to the middle of the clearing. Then paused. Then sat himself down with all the solemnity of a supreme court justice. And then began scrutinizing me from out his much-wrinkled face. Outwardly, I remained as motionless as the tree against which I was leaning. Inwardly, however, I went into a special alert, with all of my intuitive faculties as full on as possible, trying to understand just what was happening.

That monkey-squinting in my direction continued for some minutes, with neither of us making the least outer movement. It was a perfect tableau in still life. I knew at least something of his intent, as I had been through similar experiences many times before with that pal and tutor of mine, little Just Joe. I was being monkey-processed, and thoroughly so. That wild monkey was using the banana technique on me. Was reducing me to my bare essences. Was stripping me mentally naked, so that he could find out in all details what was going on back of my outer appearances. But why? I wondered.

Outwardly and conventionally observed, we were just "a wild monkey" and "a tame human," sitting in a jungle clearing and staring across at each other, with no indication as to the reason for it or what either of us might do next. Inwardly, however, I knew from experiences with other monkeys that an important ceremony was taking place between us. In this ceremony the edges of my thinking were touching the edges of his thinking, and we were contacting each other as fellow states-of-consciousness rather than as mere physical forms. We were meeting and getting to know each other in our unseen individualities—that is, in our thinking, feelings, characters, motives, and purposes. Silently, I threw into the balance my total best.

It became easily apparent that the heartbeat of that wild monkey and my own heartbeat were not only echoing back and forth, but also beginning to move in harmony and rhythm with the universal heartbeat. Without the least outer action being necessary by either of us, we were blending ourselves in a perfect mutuality of interest . . . of respect . . . of confidence . . . and of understanding. This I could feel all the way through me, and so, I knew, could he. We had invisibly shaken hands as gentlemen, so all was well with us.

Suddenly, the monkey stopped scrutinizing me. He began looking slowly around in various directions, from ground levels to tree tops. The clearing, I surmised, was a popular gathering place for wild monkeys. In that case, the monkey was a scout, and I was an intruder upon monkey territory. He had come there to investigate me thoroughly on behalf of the other monkeys that might be hiding in the neighborhood. He was to report back to his tribe. On the basis of his report, they would know how to react to my presence.

That my intuition was correct was soon to be vividly illustrated. That monkey across from me was a special scout with the gifts of a detective. As such he had given my inner as well as my outer behavior patterns a thorough going-over, from the point of view of a monkey and his fellows. Apparently, his investigation of me had yielded facts of a favorable nature. My genuine admiration, respect, and liking for all kinds of monkeys had paid off in kind. He had placed his invisible stamp of approval on me. I believe he felt certain the monkeys he was scouting for had nothing to fear from my presence in the clearing. So next, he silently "passed the word along" to the other wild monkeys in the neighborhood, telling them to come on in as they had nothing to fear from me.

Within the next few minutes the clearing became alive with monkeys. Never had I ever witnessed a spectacle like it. Nor such an assortment of monkeys. There were big ones and little ones. Old monkeys, middle-aged ones, and babies that had to be carried. Groups of them, as well as aloners. Some of them were chattering loudly, others were completely silent. They came dropping down from the trees—*it was raining monkeys!* They came leaping, walking, galloping, waddling, bounding, and skidding-in along the ground levels. Some even appeared to pop out from nowhere by special magic of their own.

Then another never-to-be-forgotten thing happened in the general excitement of it all. As the wild monkeys came hurrying into the clearing in the widely varying ways and equally different speeds, not one of them felt it necessary to give me more than a brief glance, so completely free were they from suspicion and fear. Their glances radiated confidence, understanding, and friendliness, even in their momentary contacts. They showed their individual, as well as collective, willingness to have me, a human, remain in the clearing as part of the occasion. It was a gesture that both humbled and exalted me. They had accepted me as one of themselves.

Having arrived in the clearing from their various hiding places in the surrounding jungle, the assortment of highly animated, keenly imaginative monkeys then proceeded with the much-delayed "business of the day." That "business" was first to turn their individual totalities full on, and then to establish the perfect response in knowing and doing by simply *letting the creative force of the universe flow harmoniously and rhythmically through them in fun-filled and sharing togetherness.*

CHAPTER THIRTEEN

DISTANT COLLISIONS

When it comes to the art of expressing, at one and the same time, harmony and rhythm, joy and fun, entertainment and education, monkeys, for my vote, are tops! I never tire of watching them, learning fresh living values from them, regardless of whether they happen to be imprisoned in a cage or enjoying freedom of expression in a jungle. Relatively few of the many human entertainers I have known could really educate and expand others as they did. And few of the human educators that I have watched in action were able to flavor their educating with real entertainment. But almost every monkey that I observed throughout the world was a fluid expert in blending entertainment and education.

The large assortment of wild monkeys that I so unexpectedly met in the jungle clearing was no exception. Each was an entertainer and educator in one package. The speed, agility, coordination, cooperation, and precision with which they moved themselves about was almost unbelievable. Not once as they went past, over, under, and around one another at those excessively high speeds, was there a single collision—not even a casual sideswipe. It was perfection in self-steering and in individual and group timing.

In the exciting and delightful entertainment that those monkeys put on there was not the least trace of either sameness or dullness. It was a natural, spontaneous outflow of sharable feeling and actions. *Each monkey seemed to be keenly aware that he was alive all over. Each one appeared to get maximum satisfaction out of every experience as he flung his entire aliveness into it.* They were all realistic expressions of Plato's saying that "Beauty of style and harmony and grace and good rhythm depend upon simplicity." And fortunately for those wild monkeys, none of them had been educated away from that great fact.

When I had first walked into the loveliness and stillness of that jungle clearing, its impact was so appealing that I instantly turned it into a cathedral for meditating purposes. Then into my sanctuary came all those wild monkeys, who proceeded to turn it into a circus arena. But they were more than welcome to do so, for the circus they put on for me far surpassed in real entertainment values anything that I had ever witnessed before. It was so extraordinary, as well as invigorating and refreshing, that it elevated me into a kind of sublime daze as I wondered how such things could possibly happen outside of a fairy story.

That those wild monkeys were willing to have me, a human, remain there in the clearing and watch their play-and-have-fun-time was an honor I can never forget. The more I gave thought to this, even in the midst of the exciting performance, the more understandable it became why they were doing this. Those monkeys and I had established subjective recognition between us by mentally bridging across to one another through all sorts of mental barriers. We had balanced both inner and outer interrelations as fellow beings of life. To my sense, our heartbeats were echoing back and forth in perfect attunement.

The performance those monkeys put on continued hour after hour, without an interruption or the least sag in the thrilling, amusing, and unpredictable things they did. But it was vastly more than a lot of monkeys having their kind of a pleasurable time together. It was an enchanting pageant! The superlative-plus in showmanship! It was also a rare exhibition of animated poems . . . of essays . . . of sermons . . . and of other compositions. A demonstration, too, in which all those monkeys were letting the cosmic energy and rhythm flow fully and freely through them, both for their individual and collective delight.

In the midst of that monkey frolicking and sharing there was a most dramatic anticlimax. With startling abruptness, every monkey quit whatever he happened to be doing, then swiftly looked in the same southerly direction. And then, motivated by obvious fear and panic, they went stampeding out of the clearing in a northerly direction. It was such an unexpected and extraordinary phenomenon that it knocked me for the proverbial loop, leaving me stunned and bewildered.

What had caused the sudden exodus I couldn't remotely imagine. I decided to remain where I was, with my back against the friendly tree, and see what was going to happen next. As part of this, I made myself totally alert, the way animals do. Then I began listening with all of me, the way that animals do, too. But try as I did, I couldn't mentally sniff out what had caused that sensational monkey exodus. The silence in the clearing was profound. And pervading the general atmosphere was a tense but indefinable something that was spelling t-r-o-u-b-l-e!

Three puzzling hours went ticking by. Then into the clearing from the south came five men walking in single file. The first two were carrying rifles, the other three were attendants. They were as surprised to find me there as I was to see them. We introduced ourselves. The two men with the rifles were wealthy American "sportsmen." They were making a tour of the world, shooting various kinds of wild animals to have them stuffed and sent to their homes for exhibition purposes. Their reason for coming to the clearing was "to bag some fine specimens of monkeys," which, they had been told, could usually be found there. But luck had been against them, as they hadn't seen a single monkey to take a shot at, and there were none in the clearing.

I kept silent about the unconventional experience that I had had with all those wild monkeys, preferring to listen to the hunters talk about themselves and carefully noting what each of them was mentally saying back of his vocal sounds and physical gestures. In the midst of this a most illuminating fact was revealed. At the precise moment those two hunters had picked up their rifles and headed for the clearing, three hours' walking distance away, every monkey in the clearing had fled from the place.

It was a perfect demonstration by every one of those wild monkeys in accurately hearing with the "inner ear" as well as accurately seeing with "the inner eye." And doing so as easily as breathing. Space seemed no obstacle. It was a memorable mon-key-taught lesson, too, in the simple, natural functioning of pure intuition . . . of effortless awareness . . . of correct foresight . . . and of how best to react to such intimate disclosures. And particularly interesting is the realization that the episode had taken place in the lives of an assortment of wild monkeys that had never been educated, in the conventional meaning of that term, nor had they ever experienced life outside of a jungle.

The disclosure of what invisibly must have taken place be-tween the hunters and all those wild monkeys in the clearing, when they were so far apart, gave me much to think about. Long after the hunters had started on their return journey, keenly disappointed in not finding any monkeys to shoot and have stuffed, I pondered this problem in transmission of thoughts and intents to kill. It was a vivid reminder of what takes place, either for better or for worse, when there is a clash of mental forces moving in opposite directions—no matter what the earth-riding form of the thought carriers. Species identification and the dis-tance separating physical bodies was no block to an alerted sense of survival—the genius of the reactive mind.

The essential drama between the two hunters and all the wild monkeys that had been entertaining me, I managed to unravel as follows: the instant that the two hunters began readying them-selves for their hoped-for monkey killings, they began generating a mental atmosphere toward monkeys that was sinister, cruel, murderous, deadly. They were thinking themselves into a hunt-ing mood full of destruction for "lower forms of life."

Then the two hunters picked up their rifles and headed for the distant clearing where all those wild monkeys and I were having such a delightful time—the monkeys sharing their acro-batic sense of fun, I keenly appreciative. Without being the least bit aware of the invisible forces they were setting in motion, the hunters began projecting a discordant mental atmosphere incal-culably far ahead of themselves. These states of thought were as ugly and bad-intentioned as they were destructive. Cold-blooded monkey murder was rumbling in their minds and hearts at every step they took. And the reverberations of those rumblings were vibrating far out in all directions, for every kind of an alerted inner feeling to receive—somewhat as a radio receiving set tunes in on audio air waves.

Could it be that the reverberations of the ground the cruel men were treading during their murderous mission, or the oscillation of the air they were breathing or speaking into, carried their deadly thought-quality on telekinetic or tele-audio waves strong enough to be picked up by the monkeys' built-in monitor, or radar warning system, pro-survival equipment installed by Mother Nature as an integral part of the reactive monkey mind? Did the monkeys possess a sort of survival computer sensitive enough to pick up and process vibrations of the ground and the air that sent along antisurvival messages? Could it be those messages of an animal magnetic nature travel on electromagnetic wave bands between telepathy and ordinary sense perceptions—in other words, supersensory perceptions? Who dares limit or circumscribe the infinite media of the one universal Mind?

The inevitable happened! The deadly thinking the two hunters were somehow projecting far ahead of their physical bodies crashed into the joy-filled vibrations of all those monkeys in the clearing. And while the crash was seemingly "only mental," its impact was terrific to witness outwardly. It was a major collision, even though invisible to the material senses. It was the equivalent of an explosion—an explosion in the awareness of each one of those monkeys. Two irreconcilable forces had met head-on: the antisurvival force of the hunters, and the prosurvival force of the monkeys. Every one of those monkeys knew intuitively what had caused the terrific clash and what was to follow from a killing purpose.

As I walked out of the clearing late that afternoon, still pondering what I had witnessed in long-distance mental or vibratory collisions between those two hunters and all those wild monkeys, my intellectual tailfeathers were at an all-time low, and there was much less of a human strut in me. I had been taught an invaluable lesson having to do with the potency, the sweep, and the influence of individually projected thinking, riding on invisible vibrations, be they telekinetic, sonic, electromagnetic, animal magnetic, or whatever. *How utterly impossible it is, I realized, to escape the reactions to the thoughts that one consciously or unconsciously sets in motion—even in the direction of nonhuman forms of life.* That precious and far-reaching lesson was taught me, I shall never forget, not by educated, learned, and superior humans, but by an assortment of utterly uneducated and "inferior" wild monkeys in a jungle clearing.

CHAPTER FOURTEEN

THE UNITIVE WAY

Meeting men and women in different parts of the world who were proficient in knowing how to get along understandingly, happily, and cooperatively not only with wild animals but also poisonous snakes, stinging insects, and other generally hated and feared living things, was always educational, expanding, and thrilling. Nearly all of those rare individuals were "just nobodies," but delightfully and refreshingly so—"nobodies" who liked companioning with "wild life" because of the sharing of happiness and satisfaction they got out of it. Each was participating in the same superlative achievement—that of knowing how to establish the right inner as well as outer interrelations, with every living thing they met, especially those humanly classified as "dangerous and deadly." They knew how to think horizontally across to whatever it happened to be, and then along with it, as a rational and cooperating fellow being.

As I watched those different "tame humans" and the various kinds of "wild animal" or "wild snake" associates in action, I would carefully note what each was outwardly doing, not only as an individual but as his part in the twosome. I became as totally receptive as possible, and then through the use of my "inner ear" and "inner eye" tried to identify what each of them was like and how they were functioning—in the unseen individuality—in the intimacy of thoughts, motives, feelings, character, and purposes. In their unseen individualities would always be hidden the correct interpretation for everything they were doing, or failing to do, in their easily observable withoutness.

In not one of those human-nonhuman relationship balancings that I watched had there been the slightest use of "the strong-arm method"—a popular or prevalent method for "handling animals" wherein the animal is "trained" into certain standardized behavior patterns by threats, fear, and various kinds of applied force. This blocks the animal's behavior patterns to a great extent. It disrupts or destroys natural spontaneity of expression. It hinders the animal's innate desire to understand, to be understood, to share its best, and to be appreciated. It usually accomplishes the trainer's purpose of so enslaving the animal's reactive mentality that it always moves in complete obedience to the vanity and domination urges of its "lord and master."

The "animal handling" by these delightful "just nobodies" was completely contrary to all generally practiced training methods. To those originals in human forms, the most effective way to establish total right relations with other living things, regardless of their forms, species identification, or even reputation, was first to start doing so mentally and feelingly, at the highest possible levels. They succeeded in establishing a mutuality of genuine respect, interest, understanding, goodwill, and cooperation. They let the good seed of recognition flower into rhythmical and reciprocating action. And from that blending of rhythms of hearts and minds were flowing truly amazing results in shared knowing, being, and doing.

Each of the observed participants, in those uncustomary relationship balancings, had found the cosmic link which innately holds all life together in kinship and oneness. As a result, the heartbeat of each of those humans was in tune and in time with the heartbeat of the wild animal—the snake or whatever else the creature he was companioning with. *Appreciation and love was their "magic secret" for getting along happily and well with all other living things.* None of the animals had ever wandered, or been educated away from, the great fact that life, in its real meaning and functioning, is an all-including and boundless totality, an inseparable oneness, a complete participation and sharing. And with that fact motivating and steering all, each was constantly looking for the divine and eternal in every other living thing.

With each contributing its best and trying to move in harmony and rhythm with the best within, outer unity and mutual satisfaction were established.

In a world where the mass control and manipulation of human thinking was at such peak proportions, it was reassuring to find men and women here and there who had the initiative and courage to be themselves. They were persons whose interest and compassion included every living thing they could identify. *Rather than depend upon others to do their thinking and living for them, each of those unique ones was following his inner, intuitive guidance in every least thing that he did.* When each was confronted by the common challenge of either being like all the others or going it alone, each had chosen to go it alone. And in a crowded "aloneness" each was experiencing the satisfaction and rewarding results that always come from that kind of pioneering—"far from the madding crowd," but never in want of heart companions.

Having left the broad highway of the superficial-minded, the multitudes of lock-stepping imitators of common consent, each of those unspoiled originals was blazing a unitive trail through the wilderness of his own state of consciousness—seeking that point in awareness where "all things work together for good." In those trailings and seekings, each had had to become not only a lone explorer for a season but also a lone experimentalist and discoverer every thought and step of the way. It was rarefied adventure for each one of them, far out in the generally unfamiliar where seeking becomes experience . . . experience becomes knowing . . . knowing becomes being . . . and being becomes certainty in its part in Being—in the Wholeness of Being.

Intuitively blazing those individual initiative trails hadn't been easy for any of them. It demanded unusual dedication, inner discipline, unwavering courage and vision, mental flexibility. A thorough integration of heart, thinking, character, motives, and purposes are requisites in mental-spiritual pioneering. In those unitive trailings most of them had come to discover that what appeared to be objective, or "out there," in his experience was really taking place entirely within his own individual self. Everything significant began within the boundaries of his own intuitive thinking . . . his own feelings and mentation . . . his own state of awareness—where he, and he alone, was at his own thought controls. He chose to be his own decider about everything—in central control unfolding from within. Exploring out from that basis, each was learning more and more how to move in harmonious and rhythmical interaction with all life.

The more successful I became in penetrating into the invisible motivating causes back of the visible actions of those rare men and women, the easier it became to understand why they were all such experts in knowing how to balance inner and outer relations with everything they met, especially with all forms of "wild life." Their common method was as elemental and simple as it was practical and resultful. Each of them was consistently living the best that he could, at each tick of the clock; each then radiated that best to whatever happened to be holding the attention. Always the best came back from whatever it happened to be. The interaction vividly illustrated how every living thing, regardless of its form, species identification, or level on the evolutionary scene instinctively turns toward that which is genuine—like flowers turn to the light. Perhaps behind it all stands the dynamics of growth—of spiritual progress.

As each of those pioneers moved along his own unitive trail, he was placing his emphasis for living more on the mental-spiritual than on the physical-material. He was acquiring the wisdom and knowledge that he needed from his own intuition rather than from outer hearsay and booksay. (In-tuition literally means being taught from within.) He was more interested in what he could put into life, as his part of it, than in what he could take out of life for his own personal profit. So each of them was more and more leaving the limiting personal for the expansive impersonal, the selfish for the unselfish, and the egocentric for the universal. But it was a way of life, they were all having to learn, that had to be acquired through individual effort and experience, and could not be found for them by any other person.

Another unforgettable fact about those rare individuals was that each of them had so expanded his sense of being that he regarded the entire universe as his "home." And every living thing that he contacted in his home immediately became an interesting and respected relative. But love, to them, was not a conventional human emotion or sentiment. Love, they believed, is the universal, divine Intelligence and Energy that, flowing out in its boundlessness, makes, motivates, and manages all that really is—linking all things with all things, in harmonious interrelations. Love became the unifying Principle whose dynamics are sharing.

Each of those delightful authentics had learned the same basic lesson in mastering self and the selfless skill of knowing how to establish rational and satisfying togetherness with whatever it was they happened to meet. They had learned how to tune in with the divinity in all living things—for they began to see all living things within the encompassing divinity of Love.

Love seeks and finds the mutual good in all relationships. And that lesson always pivoted around the time-honored "word to the wise"—that to experience life at its genuine best and fullest, one must love, without reservations, at his best and fullest. Each learned that to stop loving in any direction is, to that degree, to shut off the flow of infinite Life and thereby to stop living to a degree. And so each of them, as best he could, was letting the law of infinite Love flow through everything that he inwardly thought and felt, as well as what he outwardly did.

Thus was each of those humble virtuosos of life an accomplished expert in *the science and art of right relations*. They were accomplishing extraordinary, and at times impossible-seeming results. With their integrated inner world, their pure heartbeats, and their childlike spontaneity in living and loving, they were all happily operating far out beyond intellectual and orthodox routines. They were living in expanded and satisfying states of consciousness. Thus it had become possible for each of them to discover more of the real meaning of life and love. Thereby each experienced how all things belong together as rational complementary and cooperating fellow beings in the kinship and oneness of all life.

CHAPTER FIFTEEN

THE SILENT LANGUAGE

One night during my reportorial wanderings I was sitting alone in the bow of an anchored boat far down the river Nile in Egypt. A full moon was creating the superlative in gorgeous color effects. The soft, fragrant atmosphere was filled with mystery and charm. It was an enchanting place to be in and to be part of. I had returned that afternoon from an extended trip into the surrounding desert where there had been exceptional opportunities for watching rational relationship balancings between Egyptian drivers and their philosophical companions—camels, horses, and donkeys. They were unforgettable phenomena in which humans and animals had successfully bridged-across to one another intuitively, rhythmically, and spiritually.

The bow of that boat was a perfect place for horizontalizing one's feet, that is, thoroughly relaxing: to look, to listen, and to learn. So I proceeded to do just that. The more receptive I became to what was really happening all about me, the more I found myself an audience—an audience to the most magnificent symphony in color and movement that I had ever witnessed. Here was a symphony that was showing forth almost indescribable magnitudes in design, beauty, and meaning. My sensory and supersensory perceptions were moving gently but effectively through everything observable, atuned to the reciprocating rhythms of the universe.

The more I penetrated into the significance of the color symphony that was taking place all about me, the more I began recalling other unforgettable symphonies that I had been audience to in different parts of the world. They were symphonies that required neither instruments nor conductors for the fascinating results they produced ... symphonies consisting of interblending enriching thoughts, and their resultant reciprocating outer actions ... symphonies that were in perfect attunement, with the real meaning, purpose, and flow of life. They were soundless symphonies in shared being that had been produced by various individual humans and their particular artists—associates in the animal forms—a bird, a snake, an insect.

As I reviewed the fascinating symphonies in shared being between "tame humans" and "wild life" that I had been privileged to audit, I saw that all of those odd humans had used the same method in achieving their extraordinary results—in symphonic *atunement*. The instant that one of them, for the first time, met a wild animal somewhere out in the open, he would become totally motionless. So would the animal. Then the human went into effective invisible action. He did this by mentally sending his genuine admiration, respect, and goodwill across to the animal. And echoing back from the animal there invariably came its best in thinking and feelings. It was like an invisible handshake between two gentlemen—a soul-shake.

This automatically started a right balance in inner interrelations between them. A corresponding balance took place in their outer interrelations for their mutual expansion. Thus that "tame human" and "wild animal" established a unison of understanding and good purpose within as well as without. Then, in that interblending togetherness, they could move happily into the symphonic rhythms of sharing themselves in their totalities atuned to a universal key.

The "tame human" and "wild animal" got to know each other in their unseen as well as seen individualities. An awareness for the possibilities of sharing and desire to share made it easy for them to blend themselves as a twosome, suspended in a fluid mutuality of understanding, of fun, and the fullest possible satisfaction. Thus two seemingly unrelatable entities attuned themselves, their media, the cadence of pure heartbeats. *A joy-filled reciprocity of fragrant consorting on supersensory levels can rise from the cosmic harmony and rhythm that lie ever at the heart of all that really is.* Thereby both human and animal can contribute their best living tones in "the symphony of infinite response."

As I continued pondering those facts and their far-reaching implications, the Egyptian silence became even more intense and impressive. I began getting gentle inner reminders to the effect that *only in aloneness and stillness can one learn the important things about life, about oneself.* What one really needs to know is revealed in the silence that, contrary to general belief, is not a blank, but the most realistic, beautiful, and informative of all voices. It is a voice as omnipotent and omnipresent as it is intimately omniactive—a voice that is always uttering the ultimate in wisdom, knowledge, lovingkindness, and helpfulness—a voice, however, that is usually interrupted by human speaking. Vocal sounds or chatter have a way of blocking its flow. It is a voice, too, I had to learn, that can be heard only with an attentive inner ear and the childlike attention and receptivity of a pure heart. There is no sound as eloquent as complete silence.

The more I was able mentally to receive and contain what was really going on all about me as I sat in the bow of that Nile riverboat, the easier it became to identify a vast and significant meaning that was moving through that constantly changing Egyptian color symphony. Briefly summarized, it was a tangible, realistic expression of an exquisitely lovely, a flawlessly-managed universe. I had the reassurance that permeating and governing everything, everywhere, was an infinite and perfect divine Cause— the presence, the intelligence, the substance, and the energy of all that IS, or can be. Every least thing that I could identify in the surrounding Egyptian stillness and loveliness was an integral and needed part of the forever harmonious flow of the inseparable oneness of all life. Is not this a touch of Cosmic Consciousness? Can one ask for more?

Then, from out of the eloquent silence of that Egyptian loveliness, there came another gentle, revealing reminder. This had to do with "that wondrous long ago," when, according to the ancient records, everything that lived, did so in perfect understanding and cooperation with everything else. It was a period in which "the whole earth was of one language, and one speech." Could it be that long before "vanity sounds" were introduced as self-centered media that divide rather than unify, "one language" served as medium of communication, so basic and direct, it was understood by all living things? If that is so, this same universal language still lives on, deep underneath the dusty debris of the dead letter, the fallen and standing "towers of Babel" of mass miseducation, and of corrupted and commercialized mass media, fracturing society, and creating world-wide discord and universal despair.

The silent language and speech that those ancients used with all other expressions of life, I was now coming to learn in the bow of that Egyptian boat, was so simple and natural that it didn't have to be taught to anyone or anything, any more than did their breathing. They seem to have intuitively known, and had never wandered away from the fact, that *what was really doing all the thinking and communicating in each one of them was the everywhere-functioning Mind of the universe—the divine consciousness, or omniactive intelligence.*

How may modern man, frustrated from lack of meaningful communication, floundering in a dead sea of the dead letter, adrift in an ocean of conflicting words, regain again the simple medium of direct intercommunion? Is it enough to say that what the ancients were aware of is the universal Mind?

How to relate to the universal Mind is the supreme problem in media. It is constantly to listen inwardly, or subjectively. Then only can each hear, know, do and experience—each true to his inner being. The Egyptian silence whispered that everything that lived in that wondrous long ago did so with a pure, a dedicated and a universal heartbeat.

The pure in heart, those genuine originals, true to themselves, have no difficulty whatever, in communicating with one another. They know the way: they *understand media.* They also know that calm and intelligent communications, from one well-integrated nervous system to another, are the invisible yet living and reliable building blocks. Bridges across, and solid relationships that are enriching, enduring and satisfying, are built upon good communications.

It can be said that relationships crystallize along strong lines of communications, like nerve fibers along which a growing body is unfolded. Positive relationships are built on positive communications. Negative relationship or hostilities, develop along lines of negative communications.

When positive communications are forced out of a free and spontaneous flow into constricting channels, are exposed to the static of internal frictions, or are interfered with by disruptive outside influences, they may turn into negative communications. In such a case, relationships begin to disintegrate—even good relations of long standing. As this happens, people find they "get on each other's nerves," as we say in psychosomatic language.

As I pondered these deep things that trouble contemporary life, relaxed in that boat on the Nile, a fascinating correlation began unfolding itself between those ancient experts in the science and art of right relationships and the present-day demonstrators of it. By contrast, the lack of demonstration in right communications and right relationships is appallingly evident in the modern setting that has the symptoms of a disintegrating civilization.

The relationship experts look out upon life as a divinely attuned and all-including totality, an inseparable kinship and oneness. Nothing can be excluded. In interactions of boundless scope, everything has constantly to contribute its total best in order to move in harmony with everything else. Those ancients and moderns include everything they can identify in their interest . . . respect . . . love . . . loyalty . . . and cooperation.

A new day began dawning over the bow of the boat. An enchanting occasion had come to an end. I was filled with humble as well as profound gratitude—for all the fresh wisdom and knowledge that had been shared with me from out of that lovely Egyptian night and the eloquent Egyptian stillness. I felt nourished from receptivity to the eternal and divine. I had clearly and understandingly heard the Voice of Existence as it silently spoke its universal language—in the perfect cadences of endless and reciprocal being.

CHAPTER SIXTEEN

AMERICAN INDIANS

American Indians were among the most colorful and unforgettable works of living art with whom I crossed trails. Not one of
them was the least bit like the Indians one usually sees so grossly
distorted in the entertainment media. On the contrary, they were
exceptionally fine specimens, not only physically but also mentally and spiritually. What gave them special distinction was the
fact that not one of them that I talked with had permitted himself
to be either soiled or spoiled by the behavior patterns of the whitemen with whom he came in contact, nor by the ugly and viciously
bad things that whitemen had done to the Indians down through
the years in the name of "an advancing civilization."

Millions of people throughout the world have been highly
excited and thrilled by watching American Indians in melodramatic action in motion pictures, television, and other entertainment outlets. But relatively few of them, it is safe to assume, ever
learned what the real American Indian is really like, or discovered
the superb values in thinking, in character, and in living that the
Indian has to share in such abundance. What those entertainment
viewers were mostly witnessing, as well as mentally inhaling, in
those Indian-flavored productions were over-emotionalized and
over-dramatized distortions.

Another reason for the failure of the average whiteman correctly to evaluate and appreciate the American Indian, pivots
around a common paradox—that of the inability of most whitemen really to see an American Indian, even while looking at one
with their eyes wide open. In other words, the whiteman is

unable mentally to penetrate beyond the Indian's silent and shielding outer personality, recognizing his interesting unseen individuality, and so getting to know him in his totality. The whiteman has missed discovering the Indian's amazing know-how for establishing inner and outer interrelations with earth and sky and all that is between.

Yes, the real American Indian can share splendid living values in abundance. However, for years I accepted what others had said or written about him without the least effort to weigh their conclusions on my own thought scales. I had been conventionally footing-it along with the crowd-minded as just another animated carbon copy. Then came opportunities to meet Indians in their own sections of the country, to watch them in their significant individual as well as group actions. Particularly, I learned to listen to them tick mentally and spiritually back of the things they were outwardly doing, or even not doing. Thus I acquired silently taught lessons that were important to practice in my own earth-riding experience.

Whenever an Indian and I met for the first time, an invisible ceremony always took place, a ceremony that had a most important bearing on all our contacts with each other. It would begin with the Indian standing as tall, as stately, and as motionless as possible. Then from an almost expressionless face he would squint across at me. But I always knew what was going on, back of that outer fronting and squinting. With his highly sensitive intuitive faculties full-on, he was adding-and-subtracting me into my correct total. And never once did I know any of them to make a mistake in their inner as well as outer appraisal.

As a particular Indian started appraising me in this manner, I would also go to work on him. I did so by mentally stripping him down to his bare essences, with the help of my monkey-borrowed banana technique. Then I carefully noted what he was like in his unseen as well as seen individuality. This duo-action always helped us to get to know each other all the way through—that is, in our thinking, feelings, characters, motives, and purposes, as well as in what each of us had on visible display. Then as our inwardness began blending in understanding and respect, our outwardness would do so, too. And thus would we start moving along together in our totalities.

The Indian has a penetrating ability to know how to identify correctly the cause or causes back of all observed phenomena. To get along intelligently and well with a real American Indian, I gradually came to find that first of all one had to have a right balance in inner interrelations. And the foundation for this is always posited on the Indian's silent but insistent question: *"Is your heart pure, White Brother?"* If the pure heart is lacking, that ends the situation as far as the Indian is concerned. But if the heartbeat of the whiteman is genuinely pure in its tone, it instantly starts blending with the pure heart tone of the Indian. Then all becomes harmonious with him in whatever he thinks, says or otherwise does.

I carefully observed every least detail of what my Indian friend did, when he and I were together, whether he happened to be astride a horse . . . walking along a trail and trying not to harm the earth when he stepped upon it . . . or just sitting motionless and silent, in listening-and-hearing meditation. I would also try to identify the tone and significance of that which was motivating him about spiritually and mentally. This was always expanding, educational, and refreshingly different.

The more I studied with friendly curiousity the inner as well as outer behavior patterns of my various Indian friends, the more understandable it became why they were all so proficient in knowing how to blend their total best with the universal life force all about them, then move in harmony and rhythm with it. I saw why, too, they were all so skilled in carrying on effective, silent, rational correspondence with animals, birds, snakes, insects, and other nonhuman "younger brothers." One of the primary reasons for those splendid results was the fact that each was living up to his individual obligation of being a contributing member in the brotherhood of mutual usefulness.

None of those Indian friends regarded their admirable and demonstrated living values as having originated within themselves, but as reflected manifestations from what they reverently spoke of as "The Big Holy." And to them "The Big Holy" was the universal Cause . . . the Substance . . . the Intelligence . . . the Understanding . . . and the action of all that really is. So to keep in rhythm with the cosmic Plan and Purpose, each of those Indian friends was diligently looking for expressions of "The Big Holy" in every encountered living thing. They usually spoke of this individual searching as *"the great mystery"—through which,* they believed, *all have to go in order to learn individually that all life is one, and all living things brothers and sisters.*

Trying to persuade my Indian friends to tell me just what it was that they invisibly did in order to establish rational correspondence as well as outer cooperation, not only with nonhuman forms of life, but even with things growing out of the earth, was always difficult. It was not because they were indifferent or ungracious, but because they preferred to let their demonstrated results speak for them. Most of my Indian friends were of the opinion that talking, unless wisely and frugally done, causes one's power to leak away, reducing him to being just another unnecessary noise. That is why although each of them was alert and active mentally, he was outwardly traveling "the silent way." It seems that most whitemen talk as much as they can; most Indians as little as they can.

Whenever one of my Indian friends and I talked together, we usually did so slowly and cautiously, using only a few nouns, and filling in all the rest with brief hand gestures in the Indian's picturesque sign language. Their favorite method of acquiring fresh wisdom and knowledge, and especially immediately needed information, was not to seek it vocally from another Indian, or even from printed words. On the contrary, each individually went into the silence, with his silence, and then let the silence whisper to him whatever it was that he specifically needed to know. As far as I was able to find out, the silence had never once failed to cooperate with them in this manner.

One way to get expanded into a larger awareness of knowing and being is to "sit in the lap of Mother Earth" humbly with an Indian friend, look off into scenic loveliness and far distances, and *listen for the good counsel from the silence as it gently speaks to each of us in the infinite language of all life.* This language is eloquent in its boundless expression and helpful in the fresh and needed facts that are always supplied. It is a language that was never difficult for my Indian friends and me to hear and understand, providing that we were "of one mind" and listening "as one mind."

Whatever success I had in those valuable Indian-shared occasions came mostly from borrowing the Indian's effective technique in matters of this kind—that of first setting aside one's outer senses, then becoming as totally still and receptive as possible, then carefully listening to the gentle inner whisperings of infinite Intelligence as it speaks its precious wiseness from out of the surrounding eloquent silence. Thus would the Indian friend and I blend our inhearing and inseeing into a sharing knowing—experiencing together the unity and serenity of the divine Is-ness, Now-ness, and Here-ness.

CHAPTER SEVENTEEN

HEARTBEATS AND HOOFBEATS

As your thinking goes stepping along the surface of these printed pages, I would like to wave a special magic wand, mutter the right conjurations, and bring into our mutual visibility some of the exceptionally fine riders and their horses that I met in different parts of the world. Then having introduced them to you, let them put on a special show in horsemanship for us. It would be a unforgettable experience. We would see demonstrated what almost unbelievable feats humans and horses can accomplish whenever heartbeats and hoofbeats are in tune and in time.

The horseman whom I have selected to open our "magic show" is a Bedouin chief from the Arabian desert. He has long been distinguished for the exceptionally fine Arabian horses and camels that he breeds. As the chief makes his formal appearance in our "show," he is riding one of his famous horses. The picturesqueness of the chief himself, the loveliness of his horse, and their coordination in thinking as well as in rhythmical and unpredictable movements set the pace for all that follows in entertainment and education.

The second rider to be introduced is a colorful American Indian chief from the wide-open spaces of the West. He is astride an exceptionally intelligent and lively horse, moving at its topmost speed. Following them—and each rider is given a special introduction—is a charro from Mexico on his favorite horse. Then a gaucho from the Argentine. Then, one by one, some distinguished exhibitors of show horses from England, France, Italy, Japan, and the United States. Then a skilled steeplechase rider and his blue-ribbon horse from Ireland. And finally enters a hat-slanted, bow-legged, rough-riding cowboy from Texas.

In order to achieve its real purpose our "magic show" must be observed and evaluated both subjectively and objectively. In the objective, or outer phases of it, we would witness the ultimate-plus in what riders and horses can do when heartbeats and hoofbeats are echoing back and forth. This makes it possible for rider and horse to balance themselves in understanding . . . in respect . . . in love . . . in joy . . . and in fun. These qualities manifest in superb performances of "horse-man ship."

To make the subjective part of our experience effective, we need to go into a most unconventional act—that of interviewing each rider and horse after watching them in action. This can be done vocally with the human, but silently only with the horse. Also, we need to keep in the forefront of thought that *the greatest and most effective of all languages is the silent universal language of the heart. It is a language that every living thing, regardless of its form or species identification, is innately equipped with for communication.* It is a language, as all the experts in it have long pointed out, that can be spoken, heard, and understood only by the pure in heart, never by those whose hearts are impure and whose minds are mixed up.

Watching the Bedouin chief and his exceptionally fine horse perform, you might wonder—had you ever before seen such unusual horsemanship? But as we depth-interviewed each of them afterward, thereby identifying the invisible causes and links back of their visible coordinated actions, we might come into possession of their "success secret." Then we would clearly know that what we had been witnessing was a perfect balancing in inner as well as outer interrelations between a man and a horse. The chief and his four-legged associate were sharing themselves in the unheard music of motion—their common key, the indissoluble connection that ever exists among all living things.

Admiring that Arabian horse for expressing such exceptional loveliness . . . refinement . . . graciousness . . . initiative . . . and skill, in every least thing that it did, we would be in contact with a horse that had constantly been encouraged and helped to fulfill itself. That is why the purebred Arabian horse, like the one we were watching, is so greatly admired, respected and loved throughout the world.

We would also come to find that the Bedouin chief was treating his horse as a rational and cooperating fellow being—as a state of being, or consciousness, rather than as a limited biological item on four legs and conventionally tagged as "a horse." The creature was a companion, through synchronized rhythm, and a much-appreciated and admired partner in an important enterprise. The horse had as much to share as the man in their united efforts to blend their total best.

But what would probably elevate your eyebrows to hit a peak would be the discovery that the Bedouin chief, with deep humility and reverence, treated his horse as "a muluq!"—as "an angel!" Furthermore, whenever the chief prayed or meditated, he did so with one of his Arabian horses or camels nearby. This enabled the animals to become blessed and blessing companions, in their tribulations as well as in their joys.

As the American Indian chief came dashing in for his part in our "magic show," he too would be mounted on an unusually intelligent as well as highly animated horse. Then once again we would witness the seemingly impossible in horsemanship. And what would flavor the thrills with amazement and bewilderment would be the fact that the chief was riding his horse without saddle or blanket, nor did he need a bridle and reins to maneuver the horse with. How he managed to stay aboard that "naked horse" with such relaxed ease as they performed their spectacular feats was another mystery in human-horse relations.

As we interviewed the Indian chief and his horse afterward, using vocal and sign language with the former and the silent but effective universal language of the heart with the latter, we would gather in many important facts as well as some new ones worth borrowing—all about the science and art of right relations. During this we would find that the foundation for their success in rhythmical togetherness was the fact that the Indian chief from the American desert, like the Bedouin chief from the Arabian desert, had removed all possible limitations from his horse—mental, physical, and even spiritual limitations. The American

Indian was likewise sharing life with his horse as a rational, understanding, cooperating, and much-respected associate—life in motion at its most exciting. We would also discover that the Indian chief was finding great satisfaction in spending time with his horse not only as a companion and playfellow, but also as "a lodge brother." That the horse, like himself, was a member in good standing of "the brotherhood of mutual usefulness." It is a "brotherhood" in which the best thoughts, motives, and actions of each of them are kept in continuous and wise outflow, a "brotherhood," too, in which rhythmic feelings were echoing back and forth between the chief and his horse—to blend in harmonious vibrations in everything that they did together.

The chief and his horse had fused their seemingly separated "twoness" into a complementary "oneness." They were in perfect inner and outer equilibrium. They were harmonizing upon the theme of their togetherness, using their best inner tones and chords. And thus we find man and horse established for themselves a perfect balance in participating interaction . . . in reciprocal being . . . in venturesome doing . . . in precision . . . in ease of movement . . . and in the fullest possible sharing and daring.

As our "magic show" continues, we again witness the superlative and unforgettable in horsemanship by the other specially selected riders from different countries. Each horseman is wearing picturesque riding clothes and is mounted on an exceptionally fine horse. Each of them, horses as well as riders, is sparkling with vitality as well as the desire and daring to accomplish the seemingly impossible in everything that is done together. And joyfully overflowing into every least action of theirs is the fun of the shared expression of movement . . . of change . . . of thrills . . . and unbounded delight.

As we vocally interview each rider and silently interview each horse after their performances, we come upon many more illuminating facts having to do with the science and art of right relations. One of the important truths to come out of this is the fact that each of those two-leggers and four-leggers is doing his best to live in accord with the golden rule. Each is actually "doing unto the other" as he would like the other to "do unto him." They all seem to know innately, in their contacts with one another, that the golden rule always is the acid test of thought, of feelings, as well as of actions.

This practicing of the golden rule between the rider and his horse in turn makes it possible for each rider and horse to carry on silent, rational correspondence or instant intercommunication with one another. They establish between them an invisible bridge for two-way thought traffic of the reactive mind. They find, know, and experience the best in each other. And out of that flowers their rhythmical togetherness in heartbeats and hoofbeats. Thus, for each rider and horse, the floodgates of possibilities open wide— in coordination and cooperation, in unification through perfected communications. This is the Ruling Design, the Divine Plan of Central Unification ever moving through all phases of the kinship and oneness of all life.

And on that note of unfenced, coordinated and sharing togetherness our "magic show" ends.

CHAPTER EIGHTEEN

BOMBER DOG

The ability of animals, and especially dogs, to identify the motives and purposes in human thinking, even across long distances, has long provided me with fascinating but embarrassing phenomena to watch and then ponder. Fascinating, in finding out what experts animals are in instant, subjective recognition. And embarrassing, in being thus shown how far behind animals most members of the human species are in intuitive sensing, hearing, and seeing—in arriving at immediate and correct knowing without having to depend upon outer faculties or going through the laborious processes of reason and education flavored by guessing.

The more privileged I was to have animals, birds, snakes, insects, and other nonhuman fellows silently instruct me in the things I needed to know for my greater good and expansion, the more aware I became of the enriching values that every living thing has to share whenever one is ready for such an experience. But qualifying for this demands a balancing of inner as well as outer interrelations with whatever it happens to be. Then one needs to move mentally back and forth with the creature over the invisible routes of hearts and minds wherein only the best is set and kept in motion. Thus one not only experiences the harmony and rhythm of genuine togetherness, but also expands the limitations and frontiers of his awareness.

In this way, too, it became possible to establish mutually helpful correspondence with my nonhuman associate—not by vocal sounds or physical gestures, but by sharable intuitive awareness. But establishing silent good talk in this manner demands a strict discipline, especially mentally.

Dogs are expert readers of human hearts, minds, and characters, without ever being taught the valuable skill. I had this experience with all dog owners: I would be sitting in a room with a dog associate asleep on the floor. Suddenly, the dog would get to its feet, go into an intense alert, with its eyes, nose and cupped ears aimed at the entrance of the room, plainly indicating that he had mentally heard something, either good or bad, that was moving in our direction, and was readying himself for its arrival. Then, sooner or later, the invisibly identified person would visibly arrive, and in his behavior patterns would be exactly like what the dog had mentally heard and seen ahead of time.

I marveled at the precision and accuracy with which individual dogs could identify what was going on in individual human thinking, and corresponding outer actions, even across great distances. As the dog mentally "sniffed out" of the seemingly invisible whatever it needed to know about the distant personality that was holding its attention, I would mentally "sniff out" along with him, so to speak, to find out, if possible, how dogs happen to be so accomplished in this area. One of the "sniffed-out" discoveries was this: none of the dogs that I watched in those long-distant mind-reading accomplishments was handicapped by an educated and patternized intellect. Each was living in unspoiled receptivity from a basis of natural, intuitive unfoldment.

I also discovered that each of those accomplished "ordinary" dogs was operating from a much higher level of being than is ordinarily thought possible. None of those interesting four-leggers was functioning with a private and independent mind of his own. *All were reflecting the universal Intelligence as naturally and easily as they were their breathing.* They were expressing the divine Consciousness which ever includes, permeates, animates, and directs the entire universe, like individual rays of light and warmth express the sun. But this is rather difficult to grasp and understand unless one has mentally penetrated, at least to some degree, "the mist that went up from the earth."

A dramatically unforgettable illustration of the ability of a dog inwardly as well as accurately to hear and see across great distances took place during the last world war. A pilot, who had been captain of an American air squadron based in England for bombing Germany, shared this with me.

The captain's closest friend in the bombing group was a fellow navigator. Shortly after the American fliers arrived in England for the first time, the captain's navigating friend acquired a little tramp of a dog. The mutt had been doing much lonely wandering about in a country where everyone and everything were experiencing great difficulties. The little dog was starving—not alone for food, but for understanding, love, and opportunities to express and share himself. His hopes were abundantly fulfilled. He was adopted by the navigator, named Bomber Dog, and made mascot of the American flying group. The only bombings that little fellow ever participated in was in bombing everyone with his enthusiasm and affection.

The navigator and Bomber Dog became inseparable pals, except when the former had to be away on his flying assignments. At the predawn gathering in the briefing hut where orders for the day's bombings would be given, Bomber Dog would always be in attendance, lending his moral support and enthusiasm to the occasion. When the session came to an end, Bomber Dog would hurry to the long runway where he would watch each plane take off with its heavy load of bombs. Then, when the last plane was no longer in the sky, he would sadly return to the barracks and just hang around until the fliers returned.

One afternoon Bomber Dog was standing in front of the briefing hut, waiting for the fliers and especially his pal, as usual. But the little mascot was looking and acting like a different dog. His sparkle and bounce were entirely gone; he was dejected and disheartened. The first plane came in and the fliers entered the hut to report the results of their mission. But the one the dog was specially looking for was not among them. Another squadron landed, but his pal was not among them either. Then it was reported that the navigator's plane had been hit by enemy fire, blown apart, and that everyone had been killed.

For the next ten days Bomber Dog stood in front of the briefing hut, intensely watching the sky in the direction of Germany. There was a melancholy downbeat in his expression and actions. He wouldn't eat any food. None of the fliers could cheer him up or even hold his attention beyond a brief glance. The captain followed all details of the little dog's actions with studied interest, sensing that Bomber Dog was in contact with something important in the seemingly invisible that neither he nor any of the other fliers was able to identify.

Then one morning when stormy weather made flying impossible, Bomber Dog appeared in the barracks and not only resumed eating, but also played and had fun with the fliers. All was well again. The following day he was in another dismal mood, refusing to eat or having anything to do with anyone. Those unpredictable changes in moods and actions went on and on, with no one able to understand the reason for the unusual behavior. Often while in deep sleep the little dog would suddenly get to its feet, as though struck by something, and with terror in its face go into another black mood. As the puzzling phenomena continued, the captain, as much as he could, carefully watched and made notes of all phases of it.

Toward the end of the sixth month Bomber Dog went into his most melancholy mood, hiding himself under the barracks and shaking with misery. A few days later the little four-legged mystery suddenly appeared again in the barracks where all the men were. He was almost exploding with excitement and happiness, barking loudly as he could at all of them, trying to tell them something of the greatest importance that none of them could understand.

Having shared the "big news" with the fliers in the best way he could, Bomber Dog turned around and raced out of the barracks. Then, as fast as his legs could carry him, he speeded to the main entrance of the bomber base some distance away. And there the little fellow stood, just inside the gateway—barking, trembling, and almost wagging his tail off. An army truck drove in, stopping for the customary inspection. Sitting in the front seat with the driver, and grateful to be alive and back again, was the supposedly dead navigator—Bomber Dog's pal.

After the excitement had somewhat quieted down among the men at the bomber base, the captain and his navigator friend, along with Bomber Dog as a most important part of the occasion, began comparing notes. Out of it came these facts: the navigator's plane had been hit and destroyed by enemy fire, but unknown to all observers, he had managed to parachute safely to the ground. He found himself in particularly dangerous enemy territory, escape from which seemed utterly impossible. As this happened, Bomber Dog, alertly waiting for him all those many miles away in England, intuitively and accurately identified the facts. Then he went into the first of his corresponding reactions to what was happening to his pal in Germany.

Some days after landing, the navigator made contact with underground workers who provided him with a temporary safe hiding place. As this happened in Germany, Bomber Dog, in England, inwardly heard the good news, came out of his discouraged and dismal mood, began eating again, as well as playing and having fun with the fliers in the barracks. Then began the difficult effort of trying to smuggle the navigator through enemy territory. As week followed week in the seemingly impossible effort, every forward or blocked action was instantly and correctly identified by the navigator's knowing, worried, and faithful little dog pal at the American bomber base in England.

The time came when the Allied forces that were advancing through France and Belgium began bringing their line closer to Germany. As that happened, Bomber Dog began going through his most puzzling series of moods and actions. At least they were puzzling until it was subsequently learned that every mood and outer action of the intuitively far-seeing little dog was a corresponding reaction to what was happening to his navigator pal as the latter was being sneaked through enemy territory against such great odds.

After all those many weeks of extraordinary changes in inner and outer behavior, Bomber Dog came out of the blackest of them and reached his highest peak in excitement and joy. That was the day when the navigator finally arrived within the American lines and plans were made for flying him back to the American bomber base in England—back to where his understanding and faithful little dog pal was eagerly awaiting him so that they could resume sharing life together again.

CHAPTER NINETEEN

TRADE RATS

My dinner host at the Hollywood restaurant was a well-known publisher, author, and old friend then living on a picturesque estate in the mountains of Southern California that overlooked wide stretches of desert. Just as we finished ordering our food, my friend said that he had a very serious problem which he specially wanted to discuss with me—one that had been "knocking me dizzy" for some time. With his brilliant wit, which he liked to set in motion from behind a serious face, his words could have meant almost anything, or nothing at all. So with this in mind, I asked him what kind of a problem could possibly baffle him, with all that he was supposed to know, and all that his press agent was saying about him, expecting him in return to let loose his concealed joke.

"Trade rats!" he vocally flung across at me with genuine annoyance and disgust.

Then followed a bitter denunciation of trade rats, with a lengthy review of what they had been doing on his mountain estate to make life miserable for everyone. He added that while he kept killing "the things," others always sooner or later moved in, resuming the species' odd habit of carrying away valuable articles. Nothing of carryable size, belonging to him, his family, or their guests, was safe. It was, of course, a most unusual topic to discuss during dinner, but I accepted it in a spirit of new adventure.

"From what you have just told me," said I in the most impressive judicial manner I could assume, "you are not getting anywhere with your problem for obvious reasons. To begin with, you are dealing with a situation objectively, instead of subjectively. You've been concentrating your efforts on effects, in place of causes, stressing the outer and physical rather than the inner and mental. Consequently, you are intellectually upside-down, as well as inside-out! You are all fogged up by what you don't know. So naturally it's impossible for you to make anything work sensibly or successfully, either for the trade rats or yourself!"

I paused, but there being no response from my host, facially or vocally, continued. "You seem to have forgotten to remember in your trade rat dilemma," said I, "that consciousness is primary—that everything that appears to exist, as far as you are concerned, is a concept within yourself ... a concept that you have knowingly or unknowingly formed and are experiencing within your own thinking, your own individual consciousness, your own range of awareness, your specific environment. It is here where you, and you alone, are constantly bettering or worsening each concept of yours, whether you choose to call it a trade rat, a human being, or something else."

I paused again. My friend's physical body was still across from me, but where he had gone to mentally, and what he was doing there, was anyone's guess.

I resumed talking. "So there you are at your own thought controls," said I, "and what do you do? You believe trade rats to be all the terrible things that you've said they are, and have been seeing your own beliefs fulfilled, or objectified. You *expect* trade rats to enter your home and carry away valuable things, and they accommodate you in that particular, too. So why should you squawk or be confused or baffled! *You have simply been experiencing the operation of the law of expectation-and-fulfillment in action, completely overlooking the scientific fact that nothing can be corrected in your experience, whatever its nature, outside your own mentality.*"

For some minutes neither of us spoke. We had to catch up on our food intake. In addition, my friend seemed to be floundering about in a mental daze. Finally, he wanted to know how I had arrived at such a slant on things, especially in reference to trade rats.

"Some of it," I replied, " was acquired from human hearsay and booksay. But most of it came from regaining, at least to some extent, the mind of a learner and the heart of a child. As humbly and receptively as possible, I let everything that I met teach me, especially animals, birds, snakes, and insects, and even things growing out of the ground."

Each of those creatures, those nonhuman teachers of mine, I stressed to my friend, was an expert in knowing that *"thoughts are things."* They could always identify my "thought things" before I was able to express them in visible, or outer action. Every one of those four-legged, six-legged, or no-legged instructors of mine felt the impact of my thinking the instant we met. If my thoughts were flavored with genuine respect and goodwill, the equivalent would always come reechoing back from whatever it happened to be. But if there were bad elements in those "thought things" of mine, our thinking would clash, and I would usually be in for some kind of conflict and trouble.

My friend began staring ceilingward, stroking his chin as he did so, plainly indicating that he was whirling around in a mixture of interest, wonder, perplexity, and hooting questions.

Encouraged, I continued. "Trade rats," said I, "are unusually intelligent little fellows and belong to a most effective 'trade union.' Now let's assume that a number of those unionized trade rats are coming up your mountain, and there ahead of them as they turn a bend in the road, is your beautiful home. The head trade rat, who happens to be in the area for the first time, wants to know who lives in the house. The other trade rats tell him that you do. He wants to know if you are for or against them. The other trade rats let him know that you are not only against them, but murderously so.

"All right, then, fellows," the head trade rat orders, "let's go in there when they're all asleep and pack out with everything that we can carry or drag away!"

My friend laughed for the first time that evening, and on that note the occasion ended, as he had to hurry away to keep another engagement.

Late that night, sitting in my garden, I began recalling experiences that I myself had had with trade rats in different Western homes where I was a guest. Most outstanding were experiences in which, while sitting alone in a room, as motionless as the chair I was in, I would watch a trade rat in action, without in the least interrupting his plans. Those observations became increasingly interesting as I more and more began finding out about the inner and outer behavior patterns of the trade rat . . . especially its cleanliness and neatness . . . its keen intuition . . .its sparkling vitality . . . the intelligent way in which it thinks itself about . . . its rhythmical variations in movement . . . its sense of comedy . . . and especially the manner in which it "does business" with humans, who are asleep at the time.

As the trade rat made his appearance, he would have a twig or bit of something else in his mouth that he had found out of doors. Having given me a brief inspection and so evaluating me, the little fellow would start moving about swiftly in different rooms, until he came upon some bright, appealing, but not too heavy object. Then he would "close the deal" by leaving what he had been carrying in his mouth. Next I would see him carrying or dragging the object away to wherever his hideaway happened to be. A hideaway that was also his storehouse for jewelry, knives, forks, spoons and other items with the required glint and glitter to them that he had acquired through his various "trade deals."

Some months after my publishing friend and I had had our discussion about his serious and baffling trade rat problem, we again met for dinner and talk. This time his mood was entirely different. He was like an excited and happy little boy eager to share his news. His trade rat problem had been completely solved. Then he told the facts. Returning to his mountain home following our previous meeting, he and his family, as well as the help, went into what he termed "an emergency session." This consisted of a frank analysis of the kind of thinking that each of them had been doing about the trade rats on the place. *They evaluated their individual and collective thinking. They searched their thoughts concerning the law of compensation and of action-and-reaction. They concluded that one unavoidably gets back what he has sent forth in the exact measure of the sending.*

At the end of their huddle the publisher, his family and the help decided upon an experiment, new for them. They would all stop the viciously bad thinking they had been doing about the trade rats and try never again to harm them, mentally or physically. Instead, they would *look for only the best in them and expect only the best from them. Thus did they establish the law of universal love in their hearts and minds and set it vibrating in the direction of the trade rats.* Then, to their fascinated delight, *the magic rebound happened. Echoing back from the trade rats came their invisible as well as visible best.* As a result, every trade rat disappeared, and permanently so, from the publisher's lovely mountain estate. The seemingly impossible had happened! And what had brought it all about, they discovered, was simply *a change in concepts.*

Most of the fellow humans with whom I have discussed trade rats loathed and hated them with a carefully cultivated intensity. And not only that, they were killing or hiring killers for the trade rats that came into their experience. But in nearly all observed instances, they did not achieve the lasting success they desired. Consequently, a struggle ensued in which each side tried to outwit the other. But neither side seemed to be winning much of anything except more trouble.

Here and there, however, in different parts of the West, I came upon rare individual men and women who had found an effective but most unconventional way for solving their trade rat problems. Their framework for this was set in the conviction that all life is one, with a boundless variety of manifestations. *Hence, no one can possibly get anywhere at all in the science and art of right relations until he has the law of universal love functioning in his heart.* Next comes the diligent practice of this law with every living thing one meets. This enables one to establish a mutuality in understanding, in respect, and in cooperation with whatever it happens to be, even a trade rat.

That, briefly stated, was their "success secret." Those human originals, I managed to discover, were simply sending their total best across to the trade rats, and the latter were echoing back with their total best. But what those two-leggers and four-leggers were really doing, back of that uncustomary phenomenon, was *silently speaking to one another in the infinite language of Life and Love. This is the one language,* I was gradually coming to find out, *that every living thing is innately equipped to hear, to understand and correspondingly to speak.* This enables the nonhuman as well as the human to cooperate in the removal of limitations, and thereby each assumes more realistically his part in *the symphony of universal responsiveness.*

CHAPTER TWENTY

GOPHER CORRESPONDENCE

For those who don't know much about it, let it be briefly stated: a gopher is about nine inches long, broadheaded, and mostly brown-furred. Generally classified, he is a homely rodent. He also possesses many other uncomplimentary features hung on him by humans. But in spite of this low rating, he is an exceptionally wise and impressive little fellow. Life for the gopher has never been a bed of roses. Almost everywhere that he goes, humans are eager to trap, poison, or otherwise destroy him. And if some human doesn't end the gopher's career, then any hawk, coyote, snake, or fox who happens to be in the neighborhood will happily do so for eating purposes. So the gopher, of necessity, has to operate with unusual ability and agility.

With his powerful foreclaws, developed for underground tunneling, his sharp incisory teeth, and the manner in which he knows how to use them, the gopher is fascinating to watch in action. At least if one is not the owner of the garden or orchard in which the little fellow is expertly at work snapping off flowers, vegetables, young trees, and other growing things. Then, unless the gardener's feelings are under unusual control, he is apt to explode into undiluted savagery—for when it comes to wrecking gardens and orchards, the gopher is in a class all by himself.

How best to solve gopher problems effectively and permanently has long been both a headache and a challenge for countless numbers of people. The methods used for "getting rid of the nuisances" has included just about every known kind of killing process. But usually, after the killings, other gophers sooner or later move in to take the places of those destroyed. And so it has gone on and on, with neither side ever seeming to win a lasting victory.

It is rarely recognized that individual human thinking always plays an important part in human-gopher contacts. Three memorable episodes proved this to me.

The first had to do with a wealthy and prominent woman in Southern California who for many years has bristled with the firm conviction that what she thinks and says about anything is the final word on the subject, and that anyone who disagrees with her is definitely deficient in good breeding and intelligence.

While she was strolling through the formal garden of her large house one afternoon, the woman discovered a gopher at work on one of her rare plantings. Furiously angry, she began throwing everything that she could get her hands on at the little fellow. The latter ducked each flung object with perfect timing and rhythmical ease, then disappeared down a nearby hole which shortly before he had come out of. Hurrying to her greenhouse, the woman returned with a can of "guaranteed instant death poison" for all kinds of rodents. This she dumped down the gopher hole with all the murderous hatred that she could send along with it.

Early the next morning the woman hurried out to her garden to learn the effects of her poisoning efforts. Putting on her elaborately designed gold-rimmed glasses, she lowered her face as close to the gopher hole as possible for an intimate look-see. Almost instantly there was a horrified scream and the woman fell over on her side, her face covered with blood. The gopher had bitten her in the nose with his long, sharp incisory teeth. The bite was so serious that she had to be rushed to an emergency hospital. As the ambulance took her away, the gopher calmly emerged from his hole and resumed work on the rare plantings in the garden.

Through some special detective work on my part, I managed to unravel the invisible facts. Being a wise little fellow, the gopher had refused to have anything to do with the poison that had been dumped down the hole. Early the next morning he intuitively heard an important fact—that his would-be killer was physically moving toward his hole. As part of his strategy in the conflict of interests, the gopher alerted himself for action just inside the entrance to the hole. Then, when the woman's face came close enough in her hoping-for-the worst inspection, he let her have it! And how!

The second episode had to do with another prominent woman whose beautiful home has a large flower garden on one side and a particularly fine vegetable garden on the other. While she was inspecting the latter one morning, she found that a gopher had not only dug its future home under a trellis of special cucumber vines, but had done considerable damage to the vines. Instead of going into some form of outer destruction against her uninvited guest, she went into inner action. This she did by first becoming as calm and introspective as possible. Then she checked on the extent she had been living up to her cosmic obligation of always trying to identify the greatest wisdom and good in every living thing, even in a vine-wrecking gopher.

The reason for this was the woman's conviction that her gopher problem had to be solved inwardly rather than outwardly, because the entire phenomenon was taking place inside her own thinking and nowhere else. It was happening exclusively within the boundaries of her own state of consciousness. Consequently, all phases of the situation had to be worked out subjectively, owing to the fact that the objective, whatever its seeming appearance and actions, is always within the subjective and is always composed of the individual observer's own thoughts.

As the woman, with alerted intuitive listening and hearing, continued with her subjective exploring, a fact with tremendous meaning and scope began gently unfolding in her awareness. Briefly stated, it was this: she, the gopher, the cucumber vines, and everything else that she could identify were innately all of the same eternal substance, all reflections of the same infinite Source of life, all expressions of the same infinite Mind, the same all-including Intelligence. They were therefore all important and needed factors in the perfect operation of the divine Plan and Purpose.

Then it dawned upon the woman that the particular gopher ruining her cucumber vines was not the real cause for her disturbing situation. The fault was entirely her own. She had been doing bad thinking about gophers, particularly with plans of what she expected to do to gophers if any of them ever got into her gardens. She had, in the conventional human manner, been flinging detrimental thought-things at all gophers whenever they came to mind, and the thought-things, as they have a way of doing, had come boomeranging back again in her vegetable garden.

At this point, the golden rule was solidly set at the entrance to the woman's thinking, feeling, and outer actions—especially in reference to gophers in general and the one in her vegetable garden in particular. She was now aware, as never before, that her gopher problem was entirely a mental picture of her own—a mental picture that she had formulated in her withinness and was projecting into her withoutness. She saw that as she bettered her own mind picture of the gopher in the garden, the so-called outer results had to correspond, as they were aspects of one and the same thing.

There followed a balance of understanding and cooperation between them, although neither could see the other at the time. It was a harmonizing of invisible as well as visible action between those two seemingly unrelatable forms of life. It was a perfect illustration, too, of *the ancient truism that when one's heartbeat is in tune and in time with the universal heartbeat, everything that he meets will want to cooperate with him and be his friend.* The proof of this was that the gopher stopped destroying the cucumber vines, gave up his newly dug home under them, and then moved off the place. Gophers never again came into her gardens.

The third of these episodes has to do with the owner of a large estate whose special hobby is raising rare plants, flowers, and trees for exhibition purposes. He, too, had a gopher problem—one that had long been causing him trouble, anguish, and emotional explosion. In his efforts to get rid of "the damaging nuisances," he had applied all sorts of destructive methods with enthusiasm and high expectancy, only to find that after each of the killings, other gophers had arrived to resume wrecking the various kinds of valuable growing things in his gardens.

Then one day this perturbed estate owner happened to read a book that I had written called *Kinship with All Life*, in which, among other things, I told how a large army of ants had invaded my house during a weekend that I was out of town. And how, as an experiment in the unusual, I had mentally broadcast an appeal to the ants as "a gentleman to gentlemen," for their consideration and help in the situation. Then how, as a result of the appeal, every ant had gone marching out of my house. Unforgettably, this illustrated how effective such qualities as intelligence, respect and understanding can really function, even between such living items as a human and an army of ants that had invaded his house.

My experience with the ants left that estate owner dazed but fascinated. What particularly intrigued him was that as a result of my seemingly silly action, all the ants had left my house, and permanently so. Then in a spirit of childlike adventure, but in the strictest secrecy, he decided to see if he could work out a "gentlemen's agreement" with the gophers on his estate. So he sat down at his desk and wrote a letter to them, patterned after the appeal that I had made to the ants in my house. Late that night, after the members of his family had gone to bed, and in a continuing childlike spirit of adventure, curiosity, and faith, he sneaked out of his house and pushed the letter down the nearest gopher hole.

The following morning this experimenter in the seemingly outlandish went searching all over his estate to see what if any reactions there had been to his letter to the gophers. To his fascinated amazement, he couldn't find a fresh gopher track anywhere. The investigation continued daily for a number of weeks, but not the least evidence of gophers could he find, either above or below ground. Then he was convinced that the gophers had realistically understood his "gentlemen's appeal" to them and had reacted accordingly, like the "little gentlemen" they really were.

CHAPTER TWENTY-ONE

SEA GULLS

Sea gulls are experts in living the rhythm and harmony and loveliness of the Infinite in motion. I like their aerial qualities and the graceful manner in which they blend those qualities with enthusiasm, joy, and fun. And I particularly respect them for their skills of navigation in the air, regardless of whether they happen to be in headwinds, tailwinds, sidewinds, or no wind at all. I like going to one of the beaches in Southern California, either early in the morning or late in the afternoon, when seagulls are at their best. I let them teach me things that are important to know about the science and art of rising above the earth levels into higher, broader, and more satisfying awareness.

For quite a period of time on various oceans of the world, as well as along the coastlines of different countries, I had been taking special postgraduate courses in the higher education, under the tutelage of seagulls. Not once, in all that time, can I recall a dull or unprofitable occasion. What those winged instructors taught me, through the persuasive eloquence of their silent, fine examples, was always an enriching blend of entertainment and education . . . of fun and wisdom . . . and of surprise and delight. And this was so regardless of whether I was being taught by a single sea gull on the beach or flocks of them in the air.

Whenever a sea gull was in sight (and it made no difference what it was doing or not doing), school was in session and I was being taught, and well taught, too—if I happened to be inwardly, as well as outwardly, ready for the experience. So, you see, it was up to me whether anything of real value happened between us.

All that my sea gull tutor had to do at our "class time" was just be his own delightful and unpredictable self. My part, as student, was always to become totally still, like something the tide had washed in. I learned to watch outwardly, and listen inwardly, with all of me wide open.

My social and educational experiences with seagulls began on a beach at Newport, Rhode Island, where I was a small boy with a salt wave ever splashing in my face and the throb of the ocean ever in my heart. At one end of the beach, on a point of land jutting out into the Atlantic Ocean, was a farm where my family and I spent the summers. Motivated by a friendly curiosity plus a love for adventure, I spent most of my time discovering for myself the meaning and purpose back of everything that I looked at, and how to react to it. The beach was the setting for favorite adventures. There, under the promptings of my mother, I was encouraged to go exploring wherever I desired. Then I returned and shared with her what I had discovered. My mother was unusually liberal in this regard, making only one condition—that I would always return to report to her what I had experienced. Here the seeds were sown for my career as reporter. Surely, a mother is not only the strongest of educators, but can be a strong influence in determining one's career.

It was during those youthful adventures that I came to know sea gulls as much-admired relatives. I remember distinctly standing on the beach at low tide one time, eating a large homemade doughnut. I was busy puzzling out what made ocean breakers. Suddenly a sea gull landed nearby and gave me, or rather the doughnut, his interested attention. I offered him a piece of it. He walked closer and accepted it with gulping delight. Then, in mutual satisfaction, we finished eating the remainder of the doughnut together. When the sea gull eventually flew away, it carried along with it a number of my affectionate pats on its head.

What makes sea gulls so fascinating is their lovely appearance, their rhythmical movements on land, at sea, and in the air, and the valuable lessons they silently teach wherever they happen to be. With my Rhode Island background and flavoring, I also admire them for their independence—for the manner in which they do what they please, when they please, and just as it pleases them to do it. In comparison, the humans and the various animals that I knew on the farm seemed dull and limited. They couldn't, for instance, if they felt in the mood to do so, suddenly quit what they were doing, and like sea gulls, dart joyfully skyward, experiencing all sorts of exciting and satisfying fun together.

One of my long-standing regrets is that I have not been able to demonstrate a way whereby I could spread something equivalent to wings, and then accompany sea gulls in their flights. The neat manner in which they take off from the ground, their enchanting movements in flight, and their gentle landings afterward, always fill me with a mixture of admiration and envy. But while my physical body must remain on the land during those flight occasions, I can always go along with the sea gulls in my imagination. And whenever I do so, with sufficient alertness and receptivity, it never fails to be an expanding experience.

The most effective way to be taught by sea gulls, I came to find, was first to relax my physical body on the beach, then pretend I was a junior gull that needed plenty of instructing. This would get me above the foggy and swirling levels of the intellect, with its varieties of carbon-copy undemonstrable opinions having to do with how everyone else should think and act. In this way it would become possible mentally to companion with the sea gulls in the harmony and rhythm of the universal heartbeat. It would also give me a clearer understanding of the kinship of all life, wherein all life is inseparably one.

During my educational experiences under the tutelage of sea gulls I would often be reminded of a fascinating and illuminating story about the great Italian painter, sculptor, architect and engineer—Leonardo da Vinci. According to the story, Leonardo frequently went to the Tuscan fields, carrying a cage filled with birds. Reaching the best place for observation purposes, he would set the birds free. Then with his extraordinary vision and equally extraordinary receptivity, he would carefully study what each bird did in its glad upward winging. At the close of the day Leonardo would start home to resume work on his famous drawings and designs with the words, "They shall have wings!"

It is a well-known fact that this many-sided genius, called the first modern man, spent many hours on top of Tuscan hills to study the flight of birds. He was probably the first man to analyze the dynamics of flight, or aerodynamics. All that Leonardo needed to perfect the first airplane was motor power. One wonders how much of Leonardo's greatness lay in his powers of observation, patient study, and keen ability to understand the laws of nature. These laws are paraded before our eyes daily in such humble creatures as sea gulls and birds of every kind.

Sea gulls, like sailors, cannot possibly be made in calm weather. Both require lots of experience in all kinds of weather, especially the turbulent kind. This gives both sea gulls and sailors the salty flavoring they need. It also helps perfect the skills they require in having to meet their common challenge of shifting winds. The tougher and rougher the weather becomes, the more do the sea gulls like getting up into it. This provides them with exciting, fun-filled opportunities for practicing what they know about ocean and air navigation.

Whether in "airs from heaven or blasts from hell," as Shakespeare phrased it, sea gulls in flight are always superlative objects to watch, study, and then carefully ponder. And this is particularly so when those "blasts from hell" keep all shipping in the harbors, most humans under some kind of shelter, but lure the sea gulls into it for sharing adventure and fun. Then as the observer continues to watch the thrilling phenomena, he becomes filled with baffling wonderment as to how it is possible for sea gulls to do amazing precision flying under such conditions.

Another fact about sea gulls that has long fascinated me is that throughout the years that I have been watching them in flight in various parts of the world, I have never witnessed a collision between them—not even in their most sensational stunt flying in gales of wind. Nor have I ever seen a sea gull even accidentally brush the wingtip of another sea gull in their fast, close-together, and in-and-out flying. There is always precision accuracy in thinking, in timing, in navigating, and in speed management. This gave me much to ponder seriously, especially when I compared it with the shocking and almost incredible accident and death rate among humans as they attempt to steer themselves about in automobiles, airplanes, and boats.

As I became more receptive to the values that those sea gulls were silently sharing with me, I began to discover why they were all such superlative experts in navigation. They had never been taught, nor had they read any "how-to-do-it" books. The mystery of it all was as elemental and simple as it was profound.

Not a single sea gull ever operates with a private and independent mind of its own. Each is moving in harmony and rhythm with the one infinite Intelligence, with the all-embracing cosmic Cause. Each is a fluid inlet-and-outlet for all-pervading divine Consciousness. Not one of them needs any other instructing, guidance, or help in its spectacular feats of aerial flight.

CHAPTER TWENTY-TWO

THE LOVE COMPASS

Early one evening as I stopped at the home of a friend to leave a book, I walked into a fascinating adventure. My friend is a professional authority and consultant on human behavior patterns. As I handed him the book, he asked me to come in and join some of his professional friends who were having "an emergency discussion on a critical public situation." My entrance and introduction briefly interrupted a highly animated debate on the shockingly bad and worsening trends in what people were thinking and doing. As I sat down in the only remaining chair in the room, the debate was resumed with no one pulling any punches either mentally or vocally.

Because of the involved professional terms that were being used, the rapidity with which words were being flung back and forth, and the frequent interruptions in the middle of sentences, it became extremely difficult for me to keep up with them. As time went ticking along, the verbiage became heavier and heavier. So did the general atmosphere. And so did I. It finally reached such a density that I began trying to think of some tactful way by means of which I could get out into the night air again.

Just then an abrupt silence broke out in the room while most of those present lighted some form of tobacco for inhaling purposes. The man sitting to my right, and not at all in tune with the gravity of the occasion, asked the others if they had heard about the cat that a few days before had walked its way from San Francisco back to its former home in the Los Angeles area. What that started will always be a much-cherished memory.

The cat home-coming episode had been stirring up unusual public interest at the time. A woman living in the Los Angeles area who had a number of cats, gave one of them to a visiting woman friend. The latter took the cat with her to her home in San Francisco. Not at all approving of the new arrangement, and with typical catlike independence and initiative, the little four-legger slipped out of the San Francisco house and footed its way back to its former home in Los Angeles.

The conversation in the room had suddenly switched from what had to be done professionally to improve current human misbehavior, to the land-navigating accomplishment of a cat possessed with an amazing homing instinct. I couldn't resist becoming a part of the discussion, as they were now focusing their attention on one of my favorite subjects. By way of qualifying myself, I told them that for a number of years I had been a member of the Board of Animal Regulation for the city of Los Angeles. I had long been much interested in the remarkable manner in which cats, dogs, and other animals make long-distant land journeyings under their own navigation.

Most of the land-navigating animals that I managed to obtain records of had been left far beyond the boundaries of California. Their owners had moved permanently to Southern California. Weeks or months later their left-behind pets had joined them—on their own. These animals had successfully navigated themselves across those many miles of unfamiliar territory. With unfailing instinct they had found where their former human associates were living—in a city, on a mountain, in the desert, or somewhere along the Pacific coastline.

One of the most astonishing illustrations of four-legged land navigating had to do with a lovely, intelligent, and unusually affectionate sheep dog named Sally who lived with an elderly couple on a farm in southern Arkansas. Sally liked mothering everything, even humans. She mothered all who would permit her to do so. She and the elderly couple were almost inseparable. Then, in order to take an extended rest from their strenuous farm life, the man and his wife decided to go to a small health retreat hidden away in the mountains of southern California and far off all the main highways. Regretfully, Sally had to be left behind on the farm.

Early one morning, three months later, as the couple were sunning themselves on the front porch of their cottage, a gaunt dog came slowly limping down the trail toward them. Its sides were torn. Its feet were bleeding. It was swaying with exhaustion. But its tail was gently wagging. The couple stared in breathless, incredible amazement. It was Sally. Their devoted Sally! She had footed herself all the way from the farm in southern Arkansas to the hidden-away retreat in the mountains of southern California. Sally had accomplished her mission—that of finding her much-loved "Paw" and "Maw" so that she could resume taking care of them again.

While the story about Sally fascinated those professional diagnosticians of the human scene, it left them in a bewildered daze, intellectually speaking. They just couldn't figure the thing out. In the midst of their individual and collective mental whirlings, I asked them how they thought, as professional observers, it was possible for Sally to navigate herself so successfully across two thousands miles of country, and then, with unerring precision, find that hidden health retreat in the southern California mountains. I pointed out that she didn't require roadmaps or a compass, nor did she stop at gas stations along the way to ask the right directions.

There was a sanctuary-like silence in the room for some moments. Then one of the men spoke, doing so with all the solemnity of a supreme court justice who was handing down a final and irrevocable decision. Said he: "It's an instinct that certain lower forms of life seem to have and apparently know how to use upon occasions like this one." When I asked him just what he meant by the term "instinct," he looked surprised. Then he began talking in professional generalities and disappeared, so to speak, in an intellectual fog.

As a sudden change in strategy, and for whatever fun and findings might come out of it, I asked how many of them rode horses. Almost everyone present did. Then I inquired how many of them had ever been lost while riding their horses in unfamiliar territory. They had all been through that experience many times. "What do you do in situations like that?" I then tossed across to them. "Loosen the reins!" said a few. "Give the horse its head!" said the others. "What happens then?" I asked as naively and innocently as possible. They answered like a rehearsed chorus: "Why, then, the horse takes you home!"

Unsuspectingly, they had walked into my invisible trap. Having them in there, and in a spirit of inner fun but outer seriousness, I let this one go in their direction. "Gentlemen," said I, "and remember please, I am asking you as professional observers and diagnosticians, how is it that you with your 'superior brains' are unable to find your way home when lost on your horse, while your horse with its 'inferior brain' is able to take you safely home every time?"

The astonished and bewildered expressions on their faces were fascinating to watch. They had been toppled off their self-elevated ego perches and didn't quite know how to react. Perhaps it was a realistic reminder to all those savants present that only as one descends with all of himself can he really ascend to the altitude of being where he begins experiencing the universal wisdom wherewith life equips all its manifestations in the name of survival.

It was as though a fresh, salty seabreeze had blown through the room, sweeping away self-centeredness and professional strut-tings. The old combat urge, to top everyone else in vocalized opinions, was audibly deflated. A more invigorating and satisfy-ing atmosphere prevailed. As a result, everyone present sud-denly became "as a little child," and, as such, began experiencing the fun, the joy, and the superlative adventure of exploring the unfamiliar togetherness.

As the evening went rolling along, my host and his profes-sional associates began recalling truly remarkable things that they had watched various kinds of animals do. But now, with a more childlike and intuitive approach, they had come into possession of three important but forgotten facts. The first: that they had been thinking of animals as dumb, inferior, and relatively unim-portant formations, and that, consequently, they had been experiencing the results of that kind of negative thinking. The second: that all life is far greater than any of the forms that it appears to assume. And the third: that every living thing reflects an intelligence that the human intellect cannot index nor adequately explain.

And yet, certain reasonable propositions do present themselves and certain conclusions might be drawn.

What is the force that draws the lost or abandoned animal? It feels an impelling attraction to seek again the company whose dominant atmosphere was love, protection, companionship. Love, then, is the supreme attractive force. The humans who possess this capacity to love their pets must have within them a sort of love-magnet, a particular magnetic pole of affection. This may act unconsciously like a sender of love radiation. The animal, in turn, eager to pick up these love radiations, may have a built-in receiver set, as part of its reactive mind, that can be tuned in, directionally, to the source of the radiation.

Here, then, we have a magnetic pole and a compass as a minimal directional steering unit.

Another proposition is that there exist wave bands for transmitting primitive survival emotions, wave bands between the light waves utilized for physical vision and the air waves utilized in the transmission of the electromagnetic impulses translated back and forth to create televisional images on the television screen of the home receiving set.

Perhaps, again, the love-hungry animal is equipped with instinctual, reactive, prosurvival radarlike scanning devices that can pick up the direction from which the strongest love impulses are flowing toward it.

Hate being the direct opposite of love, a destructive and antisurvival force, it stands to reason that the animal radar system works also as an effective warning system. These prosurvival radar and communications systems, wherewith nature equips even her lowliest creatures, may range from telekinetic warnings picked up by miniature seismographs of extreme sensitivity that record the slightest tremors of the ground struck by enemy feet. These warning systems and media of communication are, no doubt, tied into certain sections of the animal's nervous system and may be related to electromagnetic fields.

Some of these built-in devices may scan disturbances in the ether, just above ordinary sound waves, and a possible rarefaction and extension of the sound waves. As Hamlet stated: "But this is wondrous strange! There are more things in heaven and earth, Horatio, than are dreamt of in your philosophy."

It may well be that our media-conscious age and its most advanced communication scientists, biologists, and neurologists, together with the fascinated explorers in the lush fields of extra-sensory perception, have before them fertile territories for scientific investigation. Positive findings in these critical areas may turn out to be most helpful in the planetary survival task for engineering the impending breakthrough from a materially scientific to a spiritually scientific basis of operations. Otherwise, the age seems headed toward the ultimate destructiveness of world-wide atomic fission.

It was almost dawn when our adventure came to an end. As it did so, we were all sharing a common conviction—the great importance of *becoming as a little child*." For then and then only does "the miracle" happen, and everything becomes "an open window" through which one may see and experience the Infinite One.

CHAPTER TWENTY-THREE

ECHOING HEARTBEATS

It is the man who is the missionary. It is not his words. His character is his message. In the heart of Africa, among the great Lakes, I have come upon black men and women who remembered the only white man they ever saw before—David Livingstone; and as you cross his footsteps in that dark continent, men's faces light up as they speak of the kind doctor who passed there years ago. They could not understand him, but they could feel the love that beat in his heart.
—Henry Drummond, *The Greatest Thing in the World*

The most skilled experts in the science and art of right relations that I was privileged to watch in action were basically using the same method that David Livingstone did in his famous journey across Africa. The love that beat in their hearts was as pure and fine in its essences as it was in its all-including emanations. When one has the right heartbeat—when the right motives and purposes are ticking deep within him—then everything that he meets, feeling the genuineness and worth of those emanations, will react accordingly and want to be his friend.

Many of those delightful human authentics that I came to know were experiencing comradeship and sharing and happifying adventure with "dangerous and deadly" forms of wild life that most people would have agreed should have been instantly killed, or locked up inside a safe cage. But none of them were using any of the conventional outer techniques for "animal handling." On the contrary, all were acting in a simple, natural way, after the manner of unspoiled, and so unpatternized children.

Each of these rare humans was getting maximum satisfaction out of his everyday living by being genuinely interested in every living thing that he met, and always genuinely loving whatever it happened to be, but without ever being a trader in love. They would air their total best at whatever happened to be holding their attention and interest. Echoing back from the latter would always come its total best in harmonious living tones and chords. That was the "magic secret." Through those totally expressed and sharing love actions, each of those "tame humans" and "wild nonhumans" would interblend themselves into a twosome. Then they started helping each other, to find more of the perfect beyond the imperfect . . . more of the absolute beyond the relative . . . and more of the infinite beyond the finite.

What each of those simple, modest, and highly accomplished virtuosos in the science and art of right relations seemed instinctively to know, and had never been educated away from, was that "we are all made of the same stuff eternity is made of," as Shakespeare so aptly phrased it. And with that awareness, each of them, as best he could, was constantly looking for "that stuff"— divinity, in every living thing that he met. Then identifying a measure of the eternal grandeur in whatever it happened to be, each of them would first mentally bow his admiration and respect, then diligently try to blend his indwelling divinity with theirs, for their mutual fun, happiness, good, and expansion.

This would enable those seemingly unrelatable humans and nonhumans to know each other in their unseen as well as seen individualities—that is, in their totalities. Then as pals and partners in a common enterprise, they would let the cosmic power and influence of Love flow through every least thing that they thought or otherwise did. Thus would they establish perfect mutualities, with their particular animal, snake, or human associate, in understanding . . . in respect . . . in individualized expression . . . and in sharing accomplishment. And so with their heartbeats echoing back and forth in this manner would each of those human-nonhuman twosomes not only find themselves in total harmony and rhythm with each other, but also *in rhythm with the universal heartbeat that ever pervades as well as sustains the kinship and oneness of all life—wherein all is well, always.*

Paul Herman Leonard was a close friend of J. Allen Boone, during many years in Hollywood, where Leonard was also in motion pictures, as a dancer and actor. They shared a love for writing, too.

Since World War II, Leonard has written on planetary survival issues. His articles on "Atomic Union Now" and Ideo-politics were featured in the *Christian Science Monitor* magazine section, soon after his return from the European Theater of Operations. He continues to write on constitutional and economic issues.

Additional fields of endeavor have been movement and other arts. Although he first worked in ballet companies, Leonard transcended that form to "The Classic Free Dance," after the style of Isadora Duncan. He developed "Leonard Creative Learning," consisting of dance, drama, voice, and drawing, as a basic education for all children, and sorely neglected today. Rather than consider these skills as "frills," Leonard is convinced, as were the ancient Greeks, that these arts of the body itself are basic to all higher learning.

J. Allen Boone, Paul Herman Leonard, and Emma Dunn were all close friends in those early Hollywood days. Emma Dunn was an actress of the first magnitude, working on stage and screen. Tree of Life Publications has plans to publish her book *Stand on the Divine Origin of the Constitution of the United States* together with selected writings of Paul Herman Leonard.

ANIMAL LOVERS' RESOURCE LIST

PUBLICATIONS

American Vegan Quarterly
American Vegan Society - P.O. Box 369,
Malaga NJ 08328   (609) 694-2887
www.americanvegan.org

Animal People
POB 960, Clinton, WA 98236
(360) 579-2505
www.animalpeoplenews.org

Vegetarian Times
www.vegetariantimes.com

The Animals' Voice
1354 East Avenue #R-252
Chico, CA 95926 (800) 82-VOICE
www.animalsvoice.com

Vegetarian Voice
The North American Vegetarian Society
PO Box 72, Dolgeville, NY 13329
(518) 568-7970. www.navs-online.org

ORGANIZATIONS

Animals and Society Institute
3500 Boston Street, Suite 325
Baltimore, MD 21224-5701
(410) 675-4566

Beauty Without Cruelty, USA
1340-G Industrial Ave., Petaluma, CA
94952   (888) 674.2344
(animal-friendly cosmetics and fashions)
www.beautywithoutcruelty.com.

Friends of Animals
PO Box 1244, Norwalk, CT 06856
(203) 656-1522
www.friendsofanimals.org

The Fund for Animals
200 W. 57th St., New York, NY 10019
(212) 246-2096 www.fund.org

Greenpeace, International
702 H Street, NW, Washington, DC
20001 (202) 462-1177
75 Arkansas St.
San Francisco, CA 94107
(415) 255-9221
www.greenpeace.org/usa

Humane Farming Association
PO Box 3577, San Rafael, CA 94912
(415) 771-CALF www.hfa.org

The Humane Society of the U.S.
2100 "L" St. NW, Washington, DC 20037
(202) 452-1100   www.hsus.org

Last Chance For Animals
8033 Sunset Blvd. #835
Los Angeles, CA 90046
(310) 271-6096   www.lcanimal.org

National Anti-Vivisection Society
53 W. Jackson Blvd., Suite 1552
Chicago, IL 60604   (800) 888-NAVS
www.navs.org

People for the Ethical Treatment
of Animals (PETA)
501 Front St,   Norfolk, VA 23510
www.peta.org

Physicians' Committee for Responsible
Medicine
5100 Wisconsin Ave., Ste. 400
Washington, DC 20009
(202) 686-2210 www.pcrm.org

MORE RESOURCES

Animal Rights Online Resource List
www.herbweb.org/resources.htm

Animal Concerns Community/Enviro-Link
www.animalconcerns.org

www.TreeofLifeBooks.com

Tree of Life Publications got its start with the success of this very book in the 1970's. Editor Bianca Leonardo was also the founder of the Southern California Vegetarian Society, and most of the books she published are linked to the themes of vegetarianism for health and reverence for all life. She was ordained as a minister in the Essene Church, and believed that Jesus Christ himself belonged to this vegetarian, pacifist sect.

Also by J. Allen Boone, master of silent communion and mental attitude:
Letters to Strongheart. Boone's marvelous philosophy of life pours forth in letters to his friend and mentor, Strongheart the movie dog. 243 pp, $12.
You are the Adventure. More of Boone's genial wisdom. 135 pp, $12.
Any two Boone Books, $20. All three, $25.

Acres of Diamonds: All Good Things are Possible. Inspirational Classic. Success is a result of our own consciousness. 159 pp, $8.

Books on the Essene Jesus

The Prophet of the Dead Sea Scrolls, Essenes and Early Christians. An eye-opener about what Christianity was meant to be. Jesus' ancient Essene community was morally and spiritually so far ahead of our time. Solid research from ancient sources. 174 pp, $8.

The Origin of Christianity: its Pacifism, Communalism and Vegetarianism. The perennial battle against the imperial capture of Christianity finds a valiant, sure-footed Biblical scholar in author Vaclavik. 497 pp, $20.

Saving the Savior. Analyzes all the evidence, old and new, that Jesus survived the crucifixion and escaped to teach in Kashmir. A fascinating study. Charts, photographs, bibliography. 408 pp., only $14.

The Unknown Life of Jesus Christ, Where was Jesus from ages 12-30? Follow the author's journey to Tibet to find out. 62 oversize pages, $9.

A Search for the Historical Jesus, from Asian archives. 261 pp, $17.

Christ in Kashmir. Uncanny traces of the Children of Israel. 184 pp, $14.

~ ~ ~ ~ ~ ~

Freedom from Arthritis through Nutrition. Pain-free living through simple, natural, inexpensive methods, based on decades of research. What substances to add or avoid. With 130 original recipes. 255 pp, $14.

How to Conquer Cancer, Naturally: The Grape Cure. By a doctor who cured herself from cancer thanks to the antioxidants in grapes. 96 pp, $6.

Deep Thoughts on War and Peace, by Bianca Leonardo. 52 pp, $5.

PO Box 126, Joshua Tree, CA 92252 ~ treol@earthlink.net ~ 760-366-3695